HOW TO EDUCATE YOUR CHILD WITH THE COMPUTER

A guidebook for parents

Peter Silton

Education Through Computers
Los Angeles, California
Copyright 1992

Education through Computers
A division of Unidirect Corp
11146 Montanta Ave
Los Angeles, Calif 90049

Printed in the United States of America

Distributed by Education Through Computers
Library of Congress Card Number --------------
ISBN # 1-882758-005
U.S.A.

TABLE OF CONTENTS:

PART 2   Using the educational software.

ACKNOWLEDGMENT

This book has come about as the result of the prodding of my beloved wife, Dr. Bonnie Sturner, who felt it was important that I make a contribution to society. Her words encouraged me to become involved in a mentoring program for "at risk kids." This path led into my developing an Education Center for financially underprivileged children. In order to develop the center, I found myself researching software, which became the foundation for this book.

I also want to acknowledge Judy Adelson who started me into a new career of teaching computers to individuals and Adel Martinez, Executive Director of the Neighborhood Youth Association, who helped fund the original project that developed into this book.

My thanks to Miguel Carrenza, who was my mentee and showed me what an eager boy can do when given a computer and interesting software. Without his assistance and willingness to be a guinea pig this book would not have been possible.

In each book there is the presence of the heart, mind and soul of others. This book is no exception. Without the support, opinions, advice and encouragement of a large number of people, this book would never have come into existence. The cast of people in this role is too numerous to place upon a billboard, but I wish to thank all of my friends who thought this book was a good idea and those loyal friends who understood my absence during the creative process.

And to my children; Michael, who taught me to do things on a computer that I didn't think could be done; Petra who proved to me that you could do things without a computer; Triana, who showed that there was a real need and that one person could make a difference; Tony, who demonstrated that one could learn to write and convinced me that I couldn't write, and Debbie, who demonstrated that there are people who are very intelligent, but who could use help in algebra.

In the universe of books, especially those on education, there always appear grammatical gaffes, horrendous spelling errors and embarrassing typos. No author is ever able to eradicate those completely. To the extent that this book is better than the worst or worse than the best, I am greatly indebted to Ed Kaufman who, while languishing in bed with his leg in a cast, read and reread this manuscript for grammar and punctuation; and to Triana Silton who tried to eliminate redundant, banal and inane expressions that came from my mind onto paper causing me to unpack certain sentences and expand them into chapters. And to the final editor, Cat Dale, whose red marks on my finished manuscript struck terror in my heart until I realized that there was still much to improve.

 And last to my fifth grade English teacher, Miss Yare, who sat me next to the window so I could watch the birds return in spring and at the end of the semester said in no uncertain terms, "Peter you will never learn how to write."

PREFACE

It is my belief that parents and teachers can implement a computer curriculum designed to enhance children's education. This book is written for people with little or no knowledge of personal computers. It explains everything from what type of computer to buy to how to make the best use of current technology. By providing a detailed and proven curriculum that serves as a framework for using available software, this book gives you an opportunity to help your children improve their critical learning skills. You might say this book was written with you and your child in mind.

How This Program Developed

For The Parent

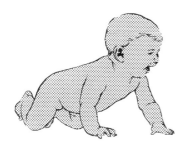 As a new father, I was constantly amazed at how much my son was learning and how quickly he grasped new concepts. I immediately assumed that he was the brightest child in the world. My bubble was burst as I saw not only my other two children develop, but how all three interacted with other children of the same age. It was not just *my* children. It seemed as if all children, given the right stimulants, had a tremendous ability to learn. This realization, enhanced by some reading on early childhood development, lead me to conclude that children are like little knowledge vacuum cleaners sucking in and absorbing every bit of information they encounter. I decided it made sense to provide not only interesting new facts for children to learn, but also intellectual stimulation in the form of new and exciting *ideas* for them to grapple with.

When my daughter was in her early developmental years, I was running a computer service bureau and had a computer terminal at home. We had a few games on the computer that I thought my daughter might enjoy, so I showed her how to play them. She picked them up so easily that I knew she would never have problems learning how to use computers. As she got a little older, I gave her a book on basic programming. In the fifth grade, she wrote a program that converted measurements in the English system to the metric system.

Encouraged by my daughter's enjoyment of the computer I actively researched existing educational software so she could use it to supplement her regular school work. There was nothing interesting available. The software was based solely on drills and rote memorization, nothing that would either entertain or keep the attention of an active child or provide her with real education. So my daughter, along with her brother and sister, were left to go their own ways with the computer, learning how to program it and, later, how to use word processing programs and other software. The computer became invaluable throughout their education. The same personal computer went from one child to the next as each one tackled college.

 My children are now grown and despite their love/hate relationship with computers they could not do their work or be who they are without them. Triana, my youngest has become a writer on a magazine called the *Ecologist* in London traveling all over with her notebook computer. My son started a business selling "shrink wrapped software for the Unix operating system." His business is completely dependent on his computer system. My stepson, who is in his second year of college just upgraded to a Mac Powerbook. He is responsible for the graphics and clip art in this book. When our children are home for visits there will be five or six computers floating about the house providing constant arguments of Mac's vs. IBM's.

About three years ago my wife suggested that I volunteer to help with the education of some disadvantaged kids. Believing that a computer consultant might be able to make a contribution to education, I volunteered my services to the Neighborhood Youth Association's Learning Center (**N.Y.A.**) in the Mar Vista area of Los Angeles. The children coming to the center for help were mostly from families with limited incomes. Many of their parents did not speak English. Very few had any books in their homes (not even a dictionary) and almost none of the parents subscribed to even one newspaper or magazine. Most of the children involved with the project didn't have a quiet place to study or do homework. They were at a terrible disadvantage in a society based on an increasingly competitive and technologically complex, information-age economy.

When I began working with youngsters at the Youth Center, I found the resources limited to prehistoric Apple computers with poorly designed educational software. Children tended to come and go within a few weeks so I had no continuity. Frustrated, but determined to find a way to help, I changed my focus from working with a group of youngsters to concentrating initially on one child.

Fortunately, within a few months of my first failure, N.Y.A began a program funded by Temple University that involved mentoring a child. I began working with Miguel, a 12-year-old with few friends, a very strict father and a chair with his name on it waiting in the principal's office. He was on a path offering little chance for success in school ...or life. As Miguel's mentor I started doing things with him in order to establish a relationship. After meeting with him for about four months, helping him with his homework and feeding pizza's to this always hungry teenager I decided to bring a computer over to Miguel's house to see how he would like it. I was astonished at how easily he learned the computer and how much at home he seemed with it. After showing him how to access its programs, I decided to leave the computer at his house for a few days. Three days later he called me to announce that he had just turned in a two-page typewritten paper using the computers word processing software. I was inspired to get him a computer so he could continue to improve his writing and other skills.

After my own children had passed through high school, I didn't pay much attention to what kind of educational software was being developed. Miguel's interest in computers prompted me once again to research the types of educational software available. I was happy to discover that the software had improved remarkably over the past decade in terms of both sophistication and focus.

Drawing on my background as a computer consultant, I made a thorough review of much of the available software and found new learning games to teach typing, math, vocabulary, composition, history and decision making. I evaluated more than 100 educational software programs and selected those that were captivating and challenging enough to hold Miguel's attention.

 With educational computer games, Miguel began to make immediate progress as measured by standard tests. He learned to type and his vocabulary and math scores shot up several grade levels. His writing, originally consisting of one-half page of barely legible writing with many misspellings and grammatical errors, expanded to correctly spelled, typewritten essays with vastly improved language structure. His self-esteem also improved immeasurably, helping his relationship with his father and his peers. In the second year of this program he became the only student from his school to ever win an award in the academic pentathlon. He also received a scholarship to a private school and found himself on the tract to college.

Miguel became the model and inspiration for the **Computer Curriculum**.

On the basis of my work with Miguel, I discussed my ideas with Adel Martinez, Executive director of the Neighborhood Youth Association. She went to the board of the Youth Center and was able to get funding to start a program of education using computers. Going to auctions and stores that sell used computers, I assembled computers and printers, desks and chairs for six students.

My classroom ready, I selected four girls and two boys, ages 12 to 15, whom I dubbed the "Computer Chips." Twice a week after school, the chips followed a step-by-step curriculum designed to teach them to type and improve their skills in math, vocabulary, composition, geography, history and decision making. They loved it. By working regularly with educational software in a logically progressive manner, the "Computer Chips" all demonstrated significant improvement. Within three months, the program had a waiting list and was expanded to include six additional students.

The kind of progress the children made was amazing. After discussing this program with different people in the community I was besieged by parents wanting me to help their children. Through private tutoring and children's workshops, I found that the curriculum worked with students from all economic and ethnic backgrounds. It was able to bridge the gap between what the public (and even private) schools are teaching and what needs to be taught to prepare children for college and productive careers.

The new software, my experience with computers, and the work I was doing with the "Computer Chips" allowed me to see the computer's potential to be used as a powerful educational tool. The students have shown me what an enormous impact computers have had on them and, with guidance, what a difference access to these kinds of tools can make in a child's life. The story of my work with these kids is also the story of how I created the **Computer Curriculum**, and ultimately how and why I wrote this book.

In the tutoring projects I worked as a teacher; but I approached my task with a critical perspective, conscious not only of how much the youngsters were learning but how well suited the computer and the software were to the learning process. My background in education was limited. My only real experience had been as a tutoring father to my three children. It was ultimately my background in computer consulting, more than my stint as tutor, which provided me with inspiration for the **Computer Curriculum**

I developed a set of goals and objectives for the program, then established a way of tracking progress, measuring results and constantly evaluating and reevaluating the program. The idea was to constantly look for ways of enhancing the children's education while keeping their attention focused on the programs. I adopted a pragmatic approach: an educational game was incorporated into the program only if it captured the children's imaginations and raised their test scores. If a piece of software didn't meet these goals, I dropped it. Using the "Computer Chips" as guinea pigs to test and research combinations of this software, the Computer Curriculum was developed. The software I recommend has been successful in allowing disadvantaged children with educational deficits to overcome those obstacles. It has also been very successful for children already familiar with computers and for gifted children . It can work for your child, too.

In order to understand the scope of this book you will need some background in the original project. Although the task seemed very complex (and it was), I was determined to find a way to help at-risk children use computers to better prepare themselves for the challenges of today and tomorrow. That included everything from helping them improve their grades to giving them better tools for the competitive job world. I believed that if I could develop a **Computer Curriculum** that would provide a significant educational advantage for at-risk children, I could develop a curriculum that could be advantageous to all children. Although rather an ambitious goal, my years in business had taught me that one can't achieve without such ambitions.

Throughout the project, I maintained (and continue to do so) a record of all the students' progress by giving them standard tests for subjects such as math and vocabulary. They were periodically re-tested to chart their progress. The improvements have been dramatic. Children have been able to raise their scores by a full grade level or more in as little as a month's time. Coming to the center at regular times, the kids have developed a sense of discipline that will help them in school, in their future careers and in their lives. Many of the students who lacked incentive in school are now motivated: they show up at the Youth Center early and don't want to leave.

Miguel now works as my paid assistant, repairing computers as well as loading and testing software. Miguel and the other "Computer Chips" long range goal is to complete high school and go on to college. One short-range goal is to develop their computer skills to the point where they qualify for good-paying jobs, as data entry or word processing clerks. Instead of working for a minimum wage at a fast food restaurant, they'll be able to earn as much as $15 per hour, enough to allow them to work their way through college.

I have written this book because it is my belief that parents and teachers will be able to achieve similar success with their children. Having read this far, you are about to take an important first step toward expanding your child's educational and career opportunities.

Chapter 1

Introduction

For The Parent

19th Century Schools Facing 21st Century Problems

Imagine you are a time traveler transported to the turn of the last century. It's amazing how different the world of 1892 would look and how antiquated life would seem. There would be no cars, only a few paved roads, a couple of skyscrapers, no telephones, no televisions, and the lifestyle of the people would seem far removed. Home life of a hundred years ago would appear primitive because it would lack many modern conveniences.

You breathe a sigh of relief as you enter the familiar school room because classrooms, surprisingly, have changed very little. The students' chairs and desks, the teacher's desk and blackboard are arranged in the same configuration as in your old school. The teacher sounds the same and is teaching the three R's in the same manner as when you were in school -- the same manner as in your child's classroom in the 1990's. You are comforted and yet unsettled as you realize that nothing has changed from 1892 to your child's classroom in 1992.

Since 1892, the only noticeable additions to the classroom might include a television set and maybe a VCR. But even these limited tools are not used to their full potential because teachers do not have access to the kinds of educational videos that would allow our children to develop the ability to learn how to be critical thinkers. Furthermore, our teachers are inadequately trained to integrate even this limited technology into their daily lesson plans, and the overall curriculum.

In viewing this comparison of schools in the 19th Century with the schools of today, it becomes apparent that there is a major problem. The society that your children will be entering, the personal relationships that govern that society, and the political structures have all changed. *In order to prepare your child to enter this new and very different world, the schools must change as well.*

Doesn't it seem extraordinary that even though the world outside the classroom has gone through major transformations, schools have remained the same? From the physical set-up of the classroom to the resources schools have accessible to them, to the way teachers present subjects, not much has changed in the past one-hundred years. Our antiquated educational system is having an impact on your child's ability to be prepared for the 21st Century.

The Role of Computers in Your Child's Life

Today is the beginning of the 21st Century as far as our children are concerned. The child who begins grammar school today will graduate high school in the next century. Of all the forces shaping the new century, none is more powerful than technology. The key tool for that technology is the computer. In the next century, we will expand our use of the computer making it central to all aspects of life.

In the United States, while we pay lip service to the idea of using computers as educational tools, we actually use them very little. In Japan, the government is committed to providing a computer in the home of every school-age child in Tokyo by the year 2000. Clearly, the Japanese recognize the importance of using computers to educate their children. They are making a commitment to using computers for education. The question for the United States is: How are we going to respond to the opportunity to use computers as educational tools?

The issue is not only the number of computers available in our schools, but the quality of education we can provide using computers as a principal tool for learning. By effectively using computers, we can help students develop the creative and problem-solving skills they will need to face the obstacles of the 21st Century.

Unfortunately, the schools of today are not in touch with our current educational needs. Teachers use textbooks, methods and curriculum plans that were obsolete before your child was even born. To provide a useful education for our children, our schools must reflect the reality of the outside world in everything from what they teach, to how they teach it. Our teachers are held back not only by the curriculums they are forced to work with, but with overcrowding and limited resources as well. The sad reality is that, in many public schools, teachers must struggle just to maintain discipline. Over-crowded classrooms and limited resources often force teachers into the role of glorified baby-sitters rather than educators.

As journalist Tracy Kidder puts it:

The problem is fundamental. Put 30 or more children of roughly the same age in a little room, confine them to desks, make them wait in lines, make them behave. As if a secret committee, now lost to history, had made a study of children and, having figured out what the greatest number were least disposed to do, declared that all of them should do it.

The best teachers are able to cope with these limitations, perhaps using some students to help each other. But even those teachers are hindered in a way that a parent/tutor working with one child and one computer is not.

Educators all over the U.S. are trying to get the educational system ready for the 21st Century. But, until they succeed, parents must do what they can to assist in their children's education, especially in the area of computers. With this tool, parents need not know New Math or Spanish to assist their child in those subjects. They need only learn some computer basics and the appropriate software to buy to help their children. This book will show you how the computer can be used in your child's education as well as ***serving as a guide for using new technology as a learning tool.***

Computers in the Schools

Chances are that your children are not learning to use computers in school. ``Not true!'' the proud parent argues. ``I know my kids have computers at their school.'' This is the same as saying that there are books in the child's school. Books are useless unless the child is taught to read them. Many factors have kept computers from being integrated into the public schools. Teachers receive inadequate training, and are not given the support they need to use computers in their classrooms. If teachers do not receive appropriate training, computers cannot become teaching tools. In addition, there are no funds allocated for maintenance of computer systems and, in many schools, more than one-half of the computers are nonfunctional.

While computers are excellent teaching tools, the potential of computer technology has simply never been realized. For children to be able to use computers, they must get basic training and spend enough hours on the computer to make the experience educationally meaningful. The sad fact is that the number of computers in our educational system is completely inadequate. Many schools don't even have a computer for every classroom. Thirty-five children are usually packed into one  classroom in a public school. At most, each child will get 30 minutes, once a week, on the computer when at least two hours, twice a week, is needed. To make matters worse, the computer equipment is apt to be terribly out of date. Most schools do not have appropriate educational software, making it difficult, if not impossible, for student's to become computer literate, much less use a computer to learn vocabulary, geography and math. The fact is, students aren't making routine use of the computer. They aren't learning to use computers as tools for thinking. Considering that more than 75% of today's jobs *require* some familiarity with computers, our children are at a big disadvantage.

Some of these problems exist even in affluent schools, where good computers are in place, because there is no standard curriculum. While it is excellent for students to learn word processing, desktop publishing, programming and advanced graphics, this curriculum fails to make full educational use of the computer.

Children love to play with drawing and animation programs; but the vocational value of those skills, excepting in the Walt Disney Studios, is doubtful. What is missing is a program to use the computer in *all* areas of school work. When students arrive at college, they need to do more with the computer than draw cartoons and put out newsletters.

People are always amazed when they hear that a student has graduated high school and still cannot read. Today we should also be appalled to find that a student has graduated high school and is not computer literate. Our schools are not helping students learn to work with the computer. We must look to other ways of doing so.

Learning to Learn

If today's students are going to compete and succeed in the 21st Century, the concept of education must be restructured. Learning, not teaching, must become the fundamental focus. Most students spend their school days as passive learners, listening to the teacher explain subject matter, copying information and answering multiple choice questions. This daily classroom routine, which might have engaged the student of the 1890's, seems hopelessly tepid and unmotivating to the student of the 1990's. Once today's students leave school in the afternoon, they are in a world dominated by electronics and computerization. Besides the ever-present television and video games, the student's world is filled with microwave ovens, cellular telephones, voice mail systems, FAX machines, bank ATMs, and a host of other tools and gadgets. For a generation used to the fast pace of MTV and video games, students find traditional teaching methods plodding. School too often seems boring and irrelevant to the technological world outside the classroom door.

To find a method to overcome this gap between education, learning and the video world, we must examine some fundamental questions.

What is learning? It seems like a simple question. Human beings start learning from the day of their birth. Some scientists believe it even begins in the womb. Dr. Diamond, a professor of Neuroanatomy at the University of California, Berkeley states that "we now have clear evidence that the environment can play a role in shaping structure and in turn, learning behavior. " One of the purposes of this program is to create a stimulating environment that will affect the plasticity of the brain.

Robert E. Slavin, in his book *Educational Psychology,* defines learning as "a change in an individual caused by experience." This broad definition covers such diverse processes as being afraid of getting an injection at the doctor's office to working out new equations in mathematics. On the basis of these examples, one could say that everybody has the ability to learn. But some must be convinced of the advantages of **learning how to learn.**

Part of learning how to learn is recognizing the major difference between undirected and unstructured learning and the type of learning that is crucial for success in today's world. The learning process that we must cultivate as we move into the 21st Century involves sorting through the vast amounts of data that inundate us and selecting the information that is important in our lives and careers. We must look for those things that relate to developments in our professional fields so that we can integrate them into our work.

Many people learn new things every day on the job, without consciously realizing it. The accountant who earned a CPA license twenty years ago has kept up to date practicing ever-changing tax codes. The auto mechanic who first began working on cars in the 1960s has had to learn about fuel injection and computer-controlled fuel systems. Likewise, the developer from the same generation has had to learn how to do environmental impact reports. These are just a few examples of the on-going educational process required in a dynamic information-age society. The student's ability to **cultivate learning as a lifetime endeavor** is the key to future success.

To be successful in the world of today and tomorrow, students do not need to memorize a maze of facts, dates and statistics. What they must do is **learn how to learn.** They must learn problem solving and how to do research. Most importantly, they must also be able to learn and understand the new concepts and products that will appear in the next century.

The Computer Curriculum

How can the education system integrate traditional teaching methods with information-age technology? This is a vital question which, for the most part, isn't being addressed. This book tackles the problem by outlining an individualized **Computer Curriculum** to help students bridge the education gap. The curriculum is balanced with emphasis on traditional subjects, such as math and geography, as well as decision-making games and exercises that foster critical thinking and creativity.

The **Computer Curriculum** will teach students the methodology to understand many of the new challenges they will experience. Working with this **Curriculum,** your children will gain valuable experience with computers. They will learn how to use technology as a tool in accomplishing their objectives while developing crucial skills for their continued educational development.

What is Education?

If you ask someone what education consists of, they may quickly answer "The three R's -- Reading, Riting and Rithmetic."

Why are these subject considered so important? They are the basic tools that we use in life. We read to find our way around, intellectually and physically. If we cannot read we are lost. (Have you ever tried reading street signs in Japan? If you cannot read the language, you literally don't know where you are.) Through writing we are able to make requests of people and explain what we are doing for them. Arithmetic allows us to solve basic problems of personal finances, budgeting and taxes. (If you don't think math is part of your daily life, try imagining what you would do at a grocery store if you had no concept of what numbers meant.) The Three R's are the basic tools that help us solve the problems of every day life.

An important new tool has arrived: the computer. Added to a curriculum focused on reading, writing, and arithmetic, computer literacy is the beginning of learning how to learn when faced with new situations.

The Four Levels of Education

Education can be structured into four levels. The **Computer Curriculum**, teaches on all four levels. Each level utilizes the processes developed in previous levels.

First Level

The first level includes the basic skills, subjects such as typing, vocabulary and the multiplication tables. These are the tools which form the foundations of our education. Our educational structure cannot be built without them.

Second Level

Subjects at this level include writing, reading, working with mathematical equations, decision making skills and solving the problems of everyday life.

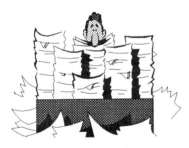

Third Level

The third level is reached when the student is taught the skill of gathering information (research), including use of the computer to access and sort through information. As John Naisbitt writes in *Megatrends*: ``... we are drowning in information but starved for knowledge.'' We must be able to access information in a structured manner. Using a computer and modem to tap into on-line data services such as CompuServe and Prodigy, one can access encyclopedias, environmental data, economic statistics, the latest news and many other facts and figures that are important for understanding the rapidly changing world around us.

There are two important advantages to using on-line services instead of doing research in the library. First, the access to information is much faster and, with better databases, more extensive than those found in most local or school libraries. Second, the computerized system is cross referenced in a way that is impossible for books to duplicate. When you first access the name of a country, the screen will display a list of related subjects. It may include the history of the royal family and the agricultural products the country is known for, along with a host of other topics. From the computer, students can enter this data base and retrieve much of the related information they need. Students can also follow a path down the ***information trail*** to discover new facts that relate to their research project, such as the incidence of a certain disease in the country. Without the structure of the data base as a frame of reference, a vast amount of information can be missed.

Fourth Level

The fourth level of education is where students develop creativity. Computer word processing and drawing programs can release the writer and artist within a student. New software will allow creativity to flourish in ways we have not yet dreamed of. Just five years ago, there were only a few visionaries in the world who could conceive of things that today are commonplace in the computer world. Some of the items which have "exploded" on the world are Desktop publishing, Fax's, and three dimensional computer assisted design. We already have software that will help us write a screenplay, a novel, or design a house. In the more purely intellectual areas, there are computer programs that will help students brainstorm and generate ideas. As technology continues to develop and the computer becomes a more commonplace tool in everyday life, we will find many new creative applications.

This book addresses all four levels of education, presenting them in parallel so that as students gain proficiency with a basic tool, such as typing (Level one), they begin to use it to tackle more complex second level subjects, such as writing book reports(level two).

Computers Can Make a Difference

The computer and a variety of educational software are the tools we are going to use to help our children. Personal computers have become a regular part of our daily lives. In the past decade hardware and software have become much easier to use, putting computer literacy within the reach of every parent and child. The new educational programs incorporate vivid graphics, high quality sound and make possible a lively interaction between student and machine. Using this book, you will learn what you need to know to guide your children using the latest software to support the educational process.

You don't need to worry about children learning to use the computer. They learn to use it faster and better than most adults. They were raised with television, VCRs and video games. The computer is a natural continuation of that technology.

In level one of the **Computer Curriculum,** students will learn the basic skills of typing, math and vocabulary. As these skills are established in their minds, students will continue on to level two: learning writing skills. Any student who learns to type using a computer will be able to write a good, legible essay in an hour. With the flexibility of computer word processing programs, the student is able to concentrate on creatively addressing a subject, letting the software check spelling and even grammar. Compare that to painstakingly writing with pen and paper. Word processing is a basic skill for writing that should be taught in school. Unfortunately, in many cases, teachers are still working with outdated curriculum. They have students memorizing synonyms and definitions instead of concentrating on how words are used to communicate. Educational success in education in America is still being measured in terms of hours spent studying, rather than looking at whether the students are acquiring the basic skills they need. Word processing is one of the skills almost all literate adults will need in the 21st century.

Level three, or the "research" level, of the **Computer Curriculum,** provides a program to help the student *learn* to learn. Learning is the ability to define a field or subject and then do research to absorb new information in that selected area. The key to learning is not to find the answer to a question in a standard quiz, but to define problems for yourself and then pose questions that are meaningful to you. This is what an accountant does when s/he asks: ``What will this new tax law mean to my corporate clients?'' The educated person today knows how to ask the right questions. Framing the questions, in terms that are meaningful to you, leads you in the direction of a meaningful answer. Notice the use of the word *meaningful*. In life there are very few *correct* answers. The world is complex. Events often have many diverse causes. Few things can be reduced to *yes* or *no* answers. This is why the true or false and even multiple choice tests still common in our schools have so little relevance to the real world of diversity and complexity.

What is Missing in the Schools

The missed potential for computers in the classroom results from a general lack of a coherent curriculum; one that would include the standard subjects for junior and senior high school: English, history, social studies, math and science. The **Computer Curriculum** supplements each of these subject areas. In English, it makes use of word processing, along with software to assist the student with spelling, grammar and vocabulary. In history it includes historical simulation games such as *Where in America's past is Carmen Sandiego?* The educational software available for math is excellent, beginning with the basics of arithmetic and working up to algebra and geometry. For science, we have programs such as *Bodyworks,* which is a complete graphic tutorial, showing all parts of the anatomy and how they function. Other programs simulate trips to Mars and scientific experiments. All of this educational software exists today and new programs are being developed and released every month.

Our educational system doesn't make use of such programs, often doesn't even take computers into consideration. Most textbooks do not assume that students have regular access to computers. Most tests do not allow students to use computers. In a world where the choices are becoming more and more complex, we are still giving true and false and multiple choice tests. In the real world, there aren't always simple *yes* and *no* answers to problems.

Tests That Teach

The educational system needs tests that not only require critical thinking, but also require formulating solutions to major problems. Educators tell us that students should learn from a test. However, it is difficult to learn much from true and false questions.

There exist "tests" that actually motivate students to think and learn. Such tests are available today on computers. The following is an example of a *learning* test.

This question deals with the reasons for the start of the second World War.

QUESTION: Which of the following do you consider the cause of World War Two?
    A.   The attack on Pearl Harbor
    B.   The invasion of Poland
    C.   Hitler's persecution of European Jews
    D.   The failure of the League of Nations to stop the rearming of Germany

This would be a multiple choice question with all the answers having some degree of validity.

If the student selects Pearl Harbor (A) as the answer, further questions would relate to the timing of the invasion of France and the Battle of Britain. Each answer would develop further questions that would point out the complexity of historical events and the multiple causes that lead to major catastrophes, such as a world war. At the end of the test, the student would be asked to write a paragraph summarizing the causes of World War II. That answer would reflect the larger view of World War II history which evolved from answering the questions. This would truly be a *learning test*.

The Parental Role in Education

In *The Unschooled Mind*, Howard Gardner reflects on the aspects of a successful education in any society. The child actually learns the most during the first five years of life when s/he is not in the educational system. During the early developmental years, the children learn at least one complete language, achieves a basic understanding of intricate patterns in human relationships and memorize a host of facts and fantasies, which in many ways are more complex than anything they will learn in later life. Gardener points out that, in many instances, an adult faced with a problem will revert to ways of thinking learned in early childhood rather than using the more sophisticated methods taught in school. Gardener suggests that if parents paid attention in their children's formative years to the kinds of skills required for success in adult life, they would change the way children are taught in school.

Gardner offers the example of a child educated in the traditional Confucian society, illustrating an education aimed at what life would eventually be as an adult in that society. Children were taught the calligraphy of the Chinese language, to play a musical instrument, to pour tea and to dress properly. These were skills the children used their entire lives. They were educated for a specific lifestyle.

In our information-age society, children need a different set of basic skills than the Confucian child, or than most of us learned in our childhood. One of the major differences between the Confucian child and your child is that no one fully knows the shape of the world your child will grow up to inhabit. The world is changing much more rapidly today than it was even ten years ago and the rate of change will continue to accelerate. For this reason, it is important for a child to learn skills that are flexible and permit change.

In the world of today and tomorrow, parents must be involved with the education of their children. The first and most influential teachers in a child's educational experience are his/her parents. In most cases, for every successful student there is a parent who reads, considers education important and is interested in how the child is progressing at school. The more stimulating the home environment and the more attention the parents pay to a child's speaking and reading skills at home, the better a child's language skills become.

Today, many parents are actively involved in their children's education, working with their children to supplement classroom learning. Parental support and direction in education will help any student.

If you had lived at the turn of the 19th Century, you would have seen fathers teaching their sons farming and husbandry. You would have observed mothers teaching their daughters housekeeping, cooking and mending.

Today, you can't teach law, business management, advertising or accounting to your children. The subjects are far too complex and what you learned in school may not be the best current thinking You can however turn your daughters or sons in a direction that will educate them for the 21st Century. ***Parents can do things that the educational system cannot.*** This book is aimed at those parents and will show them how they can help educate their children for life in the information-age.

For an example of how different learning approaches lead down different paths, we might look at an accountant, twenty years out of college who now must adapt to the world of computers. S/he might ask: ``How can I use the PC to replace my column linear pads?'' Or, ``What is the best way of understanding the functions of the PC as a tool for developing new and creative methods of business planning and accounting?'' The first question seeks simply to automate standard paper and pencil bookkeeping procedures. Intrinsic to the second question is the fact that the PC can perform multiple functions that can change one's entire approach to any field. The accountant asking the first question will probably find a way to develop a faster, more efficient method of doing what s/he has always done. The accountant asking the second question may find an answer that revolutionizes and makes all aspects of accounting faster and more efficient.

The ability of students to pose questions that are meaningful to them and move in the direction they want to go, is the key to information-age education. The **Computer Curriculum**, with its decision making programs and creative aspects, will greatly assist your child in developing this crucial skill.

The computer is not the teacher. It is the facilitator for learning. It will help develop the essential subjects and provide the possibility of creative education through individualized instruction.

Learning with computers certainly doesn't replace other types of education, but it can supplement books, teachers and parents as an additional method of teaching. Adding to and enhancing the educational process, computer learning will present educational material, such as math, vocabulary and geography in an easy to understand manner. The personal computer will increasingly be used to help junior and senior high school students learn difficult concepts.

Chapter 1 Introduction

Developing Creativity Through the Use of Special Software.(Level four)

One aspect of education lacking in today's schools is creativity. It is hard work to foster or allow creativity. It does not fit in a classroom with forty students. That type of classroom needs a tight structure with everything in its time and place. That is the very antithesis of creativity. This book will help bridge the current gap between education and creativity.

What is creativity? It is a process of free thinking that operates within a structure. Its purpose is to provide an opportunity for individual expression: in art, in writing, in acting or in any number of other ways. The process of creativity is inherently engaging and self rewarding as displayed by the concentration that a four-year-old child will put into a crayon drawing. Yet by the time students reach 5th grade this process has been removed from their curriculum. A four-year-old loves to tell stories, a ten-year-old can think of nothing to write about. At best, the fifth grader has become little more than a sponge for the teacher's lectures. At worst, the student has tuned out and is simply waiting for school to be over.

In the process of developing the computer as a tool for a child, you will have an opportunity to recreate the imaginative world of the four-year-old by giving your child the tools to be creative.

The creative process is a series of challenges faced and conquered. This is part of real life. Life is not structured like a 5th grade classroom in which chapter three comes after chapter two. Real life presents problems in a non-sequential manner, and creativity is the greatest tool for solving these problems.

Life is a continual series of challenges and problems. For some, we have "pat answers." For many, we must make decisions. For others, we must create the solution. The ability to come up with a creative solution is a key factor to successful living.

An example of a creative solution was shown by a friend of mine who was invited to visit a family in Peru for one month. His visit was scheduled for about six weeks in the future. The only problem was that the family spoke only Spanish while my friend spoke none. The "pat" answer would have been to go to a language school. However, he was working long hours and didn't have the time to spend in a classroom. He came up with a four prong solution that didn't require any additional time on his part. First, he acquired language tapes, which he used in his commute to work. Then, he explained his problem to a co-worker who spoke Spanish. They agreed to have lunch together every day for the next month and to speak only Spanish during lunch. Next, he started writing his daily journal in Spanish. And, finally, as he started to understand a little bit of the language, he watched the evening newscast in Spanish. Thus, by creative thinking, he was able to learn enough Spanish to communicate with his hosts in Peru. It was his ability to think in a creative, free flow manner that permitted him to come up with these solutions.

Computers can aid creativity by speeding up the process of trying out ideas-- ideas in words, sounds, colors or mathematical or financial relationships. This is done through *free flow* writing using a word processor or by using a computer program such as **Once Upon a Time**, which allows a child to create a picture and then write a story based on it. The child's creativity is stimulated by making something that is original and meaningful.

Creativity is an opportunity for individualized expression leading to the total involvement that students feel when they are challenged to produce something that makes full use of their knowledge and skills. Computer software can provide an environment in which greater creativity is nurtured.

Computers as Teachers to Enhance Curriculum
The **Computer Curriculum** doesn't replace other types of learning, just as books cannot replace teachers and teachers cannot replace parents. Computers can and do enhance the learning process. They are tools for teaching that can be integrated into any educational system. This book, covers the basics of education with computers. Once your child is involved with the Computer Curriculum, it can be expanded to many other areas, such as science, music, art and new concepts such as the emerging science of Chaos. Computer Assisted Learning, is a way to help your children achieve their academic goals and more. .

In the professional world today--in architecture, city planning, business and finance--computer simulation and modeling is an accepted practice. This process now needs to move into the educational system. Some software already exists which performs this type of simulation for education. Students can simulate a complex chemical experiment, take a wagon trip to Oregon, figure out real life math problems, dissect a frog, go to Mars or watch an anteater feed. Each of these simulations included multiple ``what if?'' scenarios.

The computer is an information retrieval system, a simulation machine and an idea processor. It can stimulate, challenge and delight your children. As stated before, computers will never replace teachers or parents. PCs are supplemental educational tools that become most useful when their use is supervised by parents and teachers. Working with a computer will not replace a field trip to the tide pools or to a planetarium. However, while not many students can take field trips to Mars, they can visit that planet via educational software. Technology has advanced to the point where many real life experiences can be simulated in the classroom and the home.

Areas of concentration in the Computer Curriculum

Areas where this book will help your child include:

- Typing and use of a computer keyboards and mouse (the mechanical kind) for use with all sorts of programs.

- Writing and printing reports, letters and other papers.

- Developing proficiency in math, vocabulary and other content based subjects.

In addition to the basics, this book will provide educational stimulus for:

- Developing creative projects, such as story writing and expanding the use of creative imagination.

- Using problem solving and decision making skills in simulated real life situations.

- Creating and manipulating graphic images by drawing or selecting graphics from libraries.

In learning the use of the computer as a tool, the student will develop the skills to access and interpret large quantities of information. In today's world, information is of primary importance.

The main goal of this book is to provide students with the tools and means to handle information for problem formulation, interpretation, data organization and problem solving. These are subject areas that are not emphasized enough in the classroom.

The Benefits of the Computer Curriculum

In a study done in Indiana in 1991, test data suggested that with a computer, writing skills of students increased in quality, volume and frequency. In a random sampling of fifth graders, those who were using computers wrote papers that averaged more than twice the length of papers written by non-computer users. The students in this project were typing an average of 20 words per minute, which made it easier for them to include more information in their papers. These same students spent more than eight hours per week on the computer, and even though some of the time was spent with non-educational activities, the balance was still considerably more than the non-computer students spent on homework.

The discipline of studying, doing homework and working with the **Computer Curriculum** can be instilled in a child in the sixth grade or at about the time s/he starts Junior High School. The sooner a child starts with this program the greater will be his/her accomplishments in school.

Our primary focus in this book is on children between the ages of twelve and fifteen. This book will open the mind of every child and adult to an expanded use of the computer and software. A new educational world is waiting for your child and you.

Chapter 2

Changes in Education

FOR EDUCATORS and TEACHERS

Restructuring the "19th Century Schoolhouse"

To prepare students for the 21st century, educators and teachers will have to adopt new concepts. They should be aware that educational philosophy and goals have rapidly been shifting away from traditional concepts. A new paradigm of education is coming into being. The student of today, as in the past, must be proficient in reading, writing and arithmetic (level one of the four levels of education) and must also learn the method of acquiring new knowledge. Students need to know and understand computers, information retrieval and database structure. As the world continues to change at an ever increasing rate, teachers must acknowledge that students need to know how to process new information and how to operate with new and challenging ideas. You, as teachers, need to develop the minds of your students so they can confront the changing world.

Lectures, standardized tests, grading on curves, textbooks and chalkboards are the *technologies* of choice today. In many cases those tools can no longer provide an adequate education. The harnessing of technology to assist the educator is one of the most discussed topics in the field of education. Educational software and computers have joined lectures, chalkboards and textbooks as tools of education. This book can be beneficial in helping to familiarize you, as a teacher, with the basic functions of the computer and with the best educational software available today.

Attempting Change in the Schools

In the public schools, teachers alone are hardly in the position to challenge the status quo. Curriculum committees in the schools discuss revising the accepted subjects without really addressing the idea that a total restructuring of the educational system is the only action that will allow our kids to learn. Committees on schedule changes don't address the basic question about the use of time. The terms of the debate and discussions are too narrow to provide insight into the educational process.

Every aspect of education must be reevaluated in terms of new educational goals in order to develop a new paradigm for the 21st century. This does not intimate that everything of the current curriculum must be discarded, but it does necessitate a rethinking of every aspect of education. Most educators assume that the existing building materials and architectural commitments, both physical and intellectual, will remain as they are. But, to educate for a changing world, every aspect of the physical plant and the mental structure should be redefined. We must change our own internal infrastructure and contemplate the necessary changes.

Education in Corporate America

Educators have always been cautious about new technologies, often with good reason. They do not want to *experiment* with the children they are educating. Fortunately Corporate America has had to move quickly to educate its work force to

handle the major changes in technology. Companies such as **IBM** and **Hewlett Packard** have *experimented,* restructuring employee education programs to replace a large part of their classroom training with instruction delivered by computers and telecommunications. The research compiled by industry over the last two decades shows that computer based instruction produces about thirty percent more learning in significantly less time, than traditional methods and has the flexibility to teach new and different skills. Another benefit of this format is that the overall cost for education is about thirty percent less when compared to the traditional classroom.

The use of technology as a tool to assist education does not eliminate teachers. It allows teachers to focus on individual students and to spend their time in preparing better lesson plans and tracking students' work. Teachers are no longer the "assembly line workers of the manufacturing enterprise," but now use their technological tools to become **managers of instruction,** instead of presenters of information.

Evolution of the use of computers in the school

When computers were first introduced into the schools, educators viewed them as a tool for continuing to teach the way they had always taught. This is the usual response to new technology. John Naisbitt, in *Megatrends*, talks about three stages of technological development. He says, "first new technologies follow the line of least resistance, that means they are applied in ways that are familiar and in ways that do not threaten anyone." Then, technologies are used in a way that improves on previous technologies. The first automobile looked like a carriage without a horse, and was called a horseless carriage. The first use of computers in industry was for preparing accounting ledger sheets in exactly the same format as they had been prepared for the last 50 years.

In education, this first stage (or level one) is represented by programs that "drill" basic math, spelling and vocabulary or "lecture" on other basic subjects. When technology is adapted but still uses the basic structure of the original product, the second stage, level two of the educational hierarchy, is employed. In the educational software field this stage is represented by interactive programs that use graphics and games to teach math, spelling and vocabulary. In this phase computer databases replace the encyclopedia and other research sources. An interesting example of this "second stage" is in the Central Kitsap School District in Washington. In one fifth grade class, students spend three hours per week in the school's computer lab. The teachers use the computers to "drill" students on grammar and reading comprehension. At the end of each class the teacher gets a print-out documenting the students' activities, including how long they spent and what their scores were on a particular activity. A student's next lesson is prepared with this data, permitting a teaching assistant to assign the lessons while enabling the teacher to assign individualized instruction for each student.

This format, while certainly not the ultimate use of computer facilitated education, is a big step forward from teaching to the average ability of a class rather than to the highest ability of each individual student.

Finally, Naisbitt says "new directions or uses are discovered that grow out of the technology itself." This stage of software development and computer usage have only begun to appear in education.

Teachers in schools that have incorporated some aspects of computer technology find themselves rethinking the kinds of assignments they need to give to their students. For example, one student was given three days to research demographic data on half a dozen different countries. The librarian at the school pointed the student to a computer database, and he was able to complete the assignment in twenty minutes.

At first the teacher was extremely upset, but, when she reevaluated the situation, it became clear that the student had gathered the data as assigned. The traditional concept of research as gathering information from books wasn't viable in this instance. The teacher moved the assignment up a level, asking the student to analyze the data, the objective being to formulate relationships between the data by formulating a hypothesis and fitting the data into a structure. This is a process of analysis, rather than just gathering data, turning raw data into "useful information". Research assignments by students that have access to CD ROM's and On line databases are far superior than those by students who do not have access to these resources.

In one such assignment, a student was asked to chart the rainfall and temperature of Northern Africa for the past 20 years and relate this to the food production of the area. In doing this analysis he recognized the relationship between weather (drought) and crop production. While researching some of the data on the Sudan he came across the political upheaval in certain countries and was able to integrate them into his paper. This process is a much better learning experience than only gathering demographics.

Computers, Writing and Mathematics

Computers in the classroom can lend themselves to individualized instruction in writing, mathematics and vocabulary. Writing, which is one of the cornerstones of education, has been completely changed by *Word Processing* programs. Students are able to rearrange words, rewrite and improve their papers and, in general, overcome the blocks that many youths have about writing. The computer is probably the most important new educational tool for writing since the invention of the pencil. Students can also work with educational software to strengthen their mathematical ability and to greatly enhance their vocabulary. The record keeping function, available with the key programs discussed in this book, helps the teacher track each student's progress and identify areas needing improvement. When you, as a teacher, are aware that students have computers at home, it is possible to assign homework that is an integration of the school curriculum and the educational software that is available to the student. Students could be assigned book reports and stories to be composed on a word processor. The level of homework which students produce will be superior to what they could achieve without a computer.

The Benefits: to you as a teacher

There are a number of ways that a teacher can benefit by learning to use computers. The tasks teachers perform; motivating students, managing the classroom, assessing prior knowledge, reviewing learning outcome and receiving information, can all be assisted by the computer and the proper software.

The computer can help grade students work and perform administrative duties that are a part of every school. It can eliminate a few worksheets and help in opening the communication lines between you, other teachers and administrators. Administrators can use the electronic mail feature to take attendance, schedule meetings and post announcements, eliminating the jarring interruption of loudspeakers in the middle of a poetry reading or of an attendance monitor entering the room during a student's presentation.

The computer can have another major benefit for you as a teacher by breaking down the isolation that has been such a fixture of traditional schools. Through computers you can communicate and share your thoughts with other instructors, allowing teaching to becomes a collective enterprise addressing the needs of the total student.

The role of software in teaching

Without software a computer is only a piece of machinery. The software transforms the computer into an intelligent typewriter, a spelling tutor, or an artist's palette.

In many instances a teacher will find new books or pictures to help illustrate a point in the classroom. The teacher will try to make this textbook available for the class because it will enhance the learning process. New software falls into the same category. Programs that can display the human body, show historical timelines, or perform chemical experiments are available to enhance education in biology, history and chemistry. In every field of education, programs exist or are being created that will captivate students and educate them.

Using This Curriculum in the Classroom

This book is an excellent course for training teachers to use computers as educational tools. It is an introduction to computers and educational software that also includes many advanced concepts concerning integrating education with computers. The primary purpose of this **Computer Curriculum** is to provide a guide for parents interested in doing supplemental education work with their children. However, all of the programs that are discussed here can be integrated into the classroom.

This book can serve as a resource guide to recent developments in educational software, and to the evolving world of interactive education through computers. The **Computer Curriculum** is designed for innovative and effective use of new technology. It challenges some of the traditional forms of education and, to some extent, redefines educational goals in an attempt to bring education up to date with today's needs in a rapidly shifting world. The Computer Curriculum covered in this book provides the basis for supplemental educational courses at the Junior and Senior High School level. I believe that the personal computer will lead the educational system into the 21st Century, and I know that many educators, like you, recognize its potential.

Chapter 3

The Process of Learning

For the Parent

Information Processing Theory For People and Computers

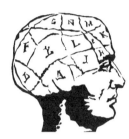

In working with the **Computer Curriculum**, we may recognize many similarities between the manner in which the computer processes, stores and retrieves data and the way your child reads, memorizes and recalls information. In this chapter, we'll discuss a well-accepted theory of learning and show a parallel with the functions performed by the computer.

Information constantly enters our mind through our senses. Much of the information we receive is not important and is filtered out. Some of it, however, is crucial for our continued well-being. For example, if a car were to come down the street at the same time a bluejay flew overhead, unless we happened to be out bird watching, we might notice the car, but pay no

attention to the bluejay. This illustrates how the mind assigns importance to some information and ignores extraneous information. It also demonstrates the bias for information that the observer brings to the scene. In this case, it is more important to avoid being run over by a car than to enjoy the flight of a bluejay.

There is a definite sequence to the method in which information is absorbed and processed. The first place information is sorted and discarded is at the sensory point, when we don't even see (sense) the bluejay for example. In a computer, the human operator fulfills the role of sensory filter, typing in data that has already been edited, with most of the extraneous information discarded.

Keys to the Educational Process

The following are major educational terms that will be used throughout this book. The terms and the concepts they represent will be helpful to you in thinking about the learning process. Let's begin with ...

... **LEARNING**: A change in an individual caused by experience. The Personnel Computer can focus an experience towards an individual and therefore impact him or her in a significant way by presenting the individual with ...

... **STIMULI**: The computer can present the student with multiple stimuli in a focused manner and in a very short period of time. It can present problems in visual and auditory manner so as to fully impact the ...

... **SENSORY REGISTER**: The first point at which a student receives information. If the importance of the information is not reinforced, the register discards it. Information told to a student in a lecture first passes into the sensory register. If it is of interest, or ties to other information that the student possesses or needs, it will continue to another part of the process. Information written on the board or into notes as well as mentioned in lectures becomes a more permanent piece of information. The student sees or hears this piece of information and has a ...

... **PERCEPTION:** How the student views the information. Not as straight forward as the sensory register, it brings our own mental state, past experience, knowledge, motivation and other factors into play. A picture of a box with one line missing may still be perceived as a box but it will get the student's ...

... **ATTENTION**: Besides perceiving information the student must be paying attention to his/her perception for it to have meaning and to permit retention. A child's complete focus and attention on a Nintendo game will demonstrate how important it is to foster that kind of intensity when the student is studying. The best educational software games engender some of that intensity which can be captured to activate the student's attention. Once the student has focused on the screen, the problem appearing there enters ...

... **SHORT TERM MEMORY**: Information processed when the student is paying attention goes into short term memory, a storage system that holds a limited amount of information for a very short period of time. When reading, it may be the specific sentence or, in math, a certain problem that is stored in short term memory. In the **Computer Curriculum** the student's attention must be focused or nothing happens. It is not the same as listening or not listening to a lecture. On the computer screen is a problem that must be committed to the student's short term memory or the learning process stops.

Another component appears in the short term memory. It consists of the definitions, interpretations and explanation that come from our ...

... **LONG TERM MEMORY:** The structure that is necessary to make sense of the stimuli we receive. For example, to make sense of the problem

$$3 \; + \; 5 \; = \; ?$$

our long term memory must report the meaning of the symbols **3**, **5**, **+**, **=**, **?** and the structure relating them. A child that has not been taught the meaning of these symbols would not move them beyond short term memory. The information would be lost. To become significant, this information must be moved to long term memory where it is more or less permanently stored. Long term memory has a very large storage capacity. Some experts believe that we never forget what is put into long term memory, but sometimes lose our ability to locate it. To retain and retrieve information, we must relate it to some other ...

... **MEANINGFUL INFORMATION**: Information that is structured and fits into a pattern. The name Niktre Evencoksn is meaningless, at least to me, whereas Kevin Costner, which consists of the same letters, clicks in my memory cells. In a vocabulary lesson, a word must fit into a structure to be meaningful. A new word becomes meaningful when it is placed in a sentence, structured with a synonym and written down in ...

 ... **NOTE TAKING**: The process of writing information down helps place it in long term memory. Simply writing the word does not place it into a structure or schema that will really make it meaningful. Add the concept of writing it into a sentence, and the word takes on a structure that helps position it. Introduce the word as a meaningful concept in a paragraph or story, and you have developed the location and association of the word in such a way that it will become substantial.

Keys to the Computer Process

To study the way the computer ``learns,'' we must consider many of the same concepts that were defined in regards to information processing by humans. The computer is limited by the amount of input it can store and/or process. In other ways though, the computer mimics the human learning process.

COMPUTER `LEARNING': The loading of a program into the computer changes the computer and permits it to perform new tasks. This is a process that begins with ...

... INFORMATION INPUT: Input is the equivalent of human sensory stimuli. A computer can get input from something being typed on the keyboard or copied magnetically from a disk. The first stop for input typed on the keyboard is the ...

... SCREEN BUFFER: The computer receives information on the screen. If it is not *processed,* the information will be discarded. If an update program is used to save the information or to relate it to a data base, the computer will update and continue to another part of the process. If the data is saved to the computer's hard disk, it becomes a more permanent piece of information. The computer reads this information as a ...

...**CONNECTION**: The computer connects the information to a program or data base. It takes a particular program that processes the new data along with accumulated data to determine the function of the new information (data base) being connected ...

...**ONE PROGRAM AT A TIME**: The computer must pay attention to the specific program it is running. Along with its connection to the data, the computer must edit information to make sure it is in the correct format and sequence. It will not permit any kind of a deviation from the proscribed formula. Each letter and space has an important meaning in computer language. Once the information has been input it enters ...

... **TEMPORARY STORAGE**: The information that is processed goes into a cache memory, which is similar to human short-term memory, until such time as it is *saved* to the hard disk. The screen buffer can hold many pages of data for ...

... **EDITING AND COMPARING**: In some programs, as data is input, there is an edit to make certain that the data is in the right format. The operating system program determines the functions of the various symbols that are input. The program recognizes numbers, knows that the symbol + means to add and that = indicates where the sum should be placed. This is possible because of what the computer has *learned.* For example it has a program that allows it to recognize and do the mathematical operation called for in the equation: $3 + 5 = ?$.
The program that tells the computer what these symbols mean is stored on the ...

... **HARD DISK**: The equivalent of long-term memory in the human brain. When the immediate process is completed in the screen, we *save* the data to the computer's hard disk. Even when we shut the computer off, it retains all the information that is on the hard disk so it is ready for ...

... RETRIEVAL: In order to retrieve information from the computer you need to have the equivalent of a map that will take you to the place on the disk where the data is stored. This "map" is the directory for the file and the file name.

Memory, Association and Recall in the Human Mind

Theorists divide long-term memory into three parts: semantic, episodic and procedural. The semantic memory operates in the same manner as a sophisticated relational data base program. Long term semantic memory contains the facts and generalized information that we know. It includes concepts, principles and rules, as well as our problem solving and learning strategies. Semantic memory organizes information into a network of connected ideas and relationships called schemata. This is similar to the organization of a data base that develops a network of connected words or symbols.

When the mind seizes on a fact, it is run through an intricate path in the brain until it hits an associated fact. Frequently, the association one person makes is not immediately evident to others. For example, someone interested in Buddhism might look at a snow capped mountain and think of the Dali Lama, the exiled spiritual leader of Tibet. (Meanwhile, a literary buff might think of Ernest Hemingway and his famous short story *The Snows of Kilimanjaro*.) Thinking of the Dali Lama's long struggle against Chinese repression might lead to associations with the United Nations and international groups dedicated to ending religious persecution and human rights abuses. This illustrates how a chain of unstructured associations triggers our memories.

Data Bases, Associations and Retrieval in Computers

Computers cannot make the cryptic associations the human mind is capable of. They have to use a data base structure to link related facts using key words. In a data base, information about the Dali Lama might be linked to keywords including *Tibet, China, Buddhism* and *human rights*. A person could define these keywords and set up the structure as information about the Dali Lama was input into the computer.

There are, however, a few data base programs that allow data to be entered first and linked together with keywords later. As these programs become more sophisticated and more common, the analogy between humans and computers is strengthened. Of course, the human brain is still far more complex and flexible. Our minds are constantly taking in data and building associations afterwards. Meanwhile, programs such as *LOTUS AGENDA* can build a data base after the fact, but still work within a limited and formalized structure. There is a vast difference between the schematic associations of the human mind and even the best computer data base software.

The Computer as an Electronic Tutor

Viewing the parallels of learning between humans and computers shows how computer systems can be employed as electronic tutors. The process and structure of storing and retrieving information, structuring data and processing it, as done by well-designed software, is closely related to how a child learns. Information presented in an attention riveting fashion with the related structure puts the whole process into an easily absorbed form.

For example, a word presented in *Word Attack Plus* (a vocabulary teaching program) is presented in five different ways and in two structured relationships. A student who has processed those words has a complete set of relationships to the meaning of the words.

In the program ***Where in the World is Carmen Sandiego?*** there are clues relating economic, geographic or political relationships to a specific place in the world. The data base for each country is developed by displaying clues about currency such as Franc for France, geographic features like Mt. Everest for Nepal and man made structures such as the pyramids for Egypt.

In ***Math Blaster Mystery*** (a problem solving math program) problems are analyzed and the important facts determined. It develops the concept of selecting key information and excluding extraneous data.

Once you have worked with your child on the **Computer Curriculum**, you will recognize many of the processes of learning and see how they can be very beneficial for all aspects of his/her academic life and career.

Chapter 4

Buying a Computer

EDITOR'S NOTE: This section is devoted to parents who need to purchase a personal computer for this program. If you already own a computer, proceed to the section on upgrades to determine if your system can run the educational software recommended in this book.

For the Parent

Buying a computer today can be a harrowing experience. The choices are often confusing and the language is unfamiliar. Salespeople want to know how many megahertz you need and what your VGA is while you're still trying to figure out who **Ms. Dos** is. To help you through this confusing process, the following is a list of definitions of common computer terms and a description of specific system requirements. A basic knowledge of these terms will help you proceed to a computer store and purchase the computer most suited to your needs.

Ms Dos

Glossary of Terms

Some common computer terms and definitions:

microchips: Microchips have a variety of uses, including their function as the brains of the computer. They are made of silicon pieces about a quarter inch square and contain millions of electrical components.

types of microchips: The central processing chip in a Personal Computer(PC) is often referred to by numbers. In the old IBM PC-AT, the chip was 80286. Computer jargon simplifies the code number, dropping the 80, and machines are simply referred to as the last three digits of the code number. Machines are called 286's, 386's and now 486's; the higher the number, the more powerful the computer.

motherboard: The main circuit board of a computer. It contains the connectors for attaching other boards. The CPU, (Central Processing Unit) memory, ports and controllers are usually on that board.

cache memory: A high speed storage mechanism usually related to memory. It is not as fast as memory but considerably faster than disk storage.

laptop: Easy definition -- a portable computer small enough to fit on your lap. These machines, weighing between nine and 12 pounds, became popular in the late 80's and early 90's. They can now be purchased relatively inexpensively because they are being replaced in popularity by the even smaller notebook computers.

notebook: This computer is literally the size of a notebook. It weighs between five and a half and eight pounds and usually comes with a 3 1/2-inch floppy disk drive and a 40 to 60 megabyte hard disk. It can be purchased with a color monitor, but they are still fairly costly.

floppy disk drive: A disk drive that reads data and program information stored magnetically on a floppy disk(these disks are not always "floppy" but are sometimes hard.) Disk drives are of two basic sizes: 5 1/4-inch and 3 1/2-inch. Placing floppy disks into the computer is similar to loading a tape into a cassette player. The floppy disk drive allows the computer to run the program recorded on the disk, which you can then copy onto the hard disk drive of the computer.

hard disk drive: These are high capacity disk drives built into the computer. If you copy a program from your floppy disk to the hard disk, it is permanently resident in the computer. You can run a program stored on the hard disk without having to load it from a floppy disks. Hard disk drives are designated by numbers representing their storage capacity in megabytes. A 20 megabyte hard disk is the smallest. The numbers go to 40, 60 and 105 megabytes and higher. Because so many programs today take large amounts of storage space, bigger is usually better.

monochrome monitor: The computer display screen that is roughly equivalent to a black and white television. Actually, a monochrome monitor has two contrasting colors, a dark color background with light numbers and letters or vice versa.

RGB monitor: The earliest color monitor using primary colors: Red, Green and Blue. It is very difficult to read text on an RGB monitor

CGA monitor: Color Graphic Adapter, now obsolete. The clarity is not good enough for extended writing.

EGA monitor: Enhanced Graphics Adapter. This is an improvement over CGA but is only fair for text.

VGA monitor: Video Graphics Adapter. This offers much better resolution which will be critical for a student using the computer for long writing and math projects.

Super VGA monitor: Even better than VGA. This is the one to buy. The cost of this type of monitor is dropping rapidly.

connectors on cables: A connector (similar to an electric outlet plug) at the end of a cable that allows you to hook a printer or mouse to the computer.

ports: The receptacles in the back of the computer where you plug in the cable connectors.

Buying a Computer

The past five years have seen a tremendous development in hardware. The colors that can be displayed on the screen grew from 16 to 256 and on to 16,000. Computer memory increased from 640 kb to 8 mb. Hard disk capacity jumped from 20 megabytes (or about 1000 pages) to 105 mb (or about 5000 pages) and even higher capacity disk drives are now being offered. When these advances were first introduced, the prices were prohibitive except for computer experts and companies with a strong business reason for upgrading. Now, however, prices are reasonable and dropping weekly. This does not imply that you should delay purchasing your computer system. The sooner your children start, the greater benefits they will obtain.

The decline in prices makes personal computers affordable for many families, but I do have some words of caution. The development of new technology happened so quickly that many stores still have computers in stock featuring what is out-moded technology. Beware of the salesman who offers you an incredible bargain on a name-brand computer. It may be a computer that will meet your specific needs at a terrific price or it may be an obsolete system that won't run the programs you will want to  use. Make sure the computer has all of the features we will list in appendix A before making your purchase. You want to buy a computer that will take full advantage of the capabilities of the educational software.

Making a Purchase

As you walk into a well-stocked computer store, your eyes will widen while eager salespeople demonstrate the latest and greatest awesome array of technology. It is easy to get caught up in the hype and lose sight of what you came to buy. To avoid sales pressure, tell the salesperson exactly what you want based on the system requirements listed in this chapter. Then, listen carefully to what the salesman says because there may be new features that you want to include in your purchase.

I don't recommend buying from a major department store or discount house. They usually don't have anyone on staff with any expertise in computers, so you won't be able to get support if you have any problems.

There are many discount computer stores in all major cities and the mail order channel has been very successful. Some mail order houses have built excellent reputations for service and price. Ads for these mail order houses can be found in *PC World, PC Computing* and other major PC magazines on the newsstand.

There is also a magazine called **Computer Shopper** which has interesting articles and also an extensive list of mail order items. If you feel that you can set up the computer on your own by following the manual directions, mail order is a very price effective method of purchasing a system.

If you want to *feel* safe, stick to brand names such as IBM, Dell, Compaq or AST. If you do this, you should know that you will probably be paying a little more. In today's highly competitive market, many of the lesser known brands are as reliable as the systems from the major manufacturers. Make certain the store or mail order house you purchase from will stand behind its product.

What to Look for in a Basic Computer System

When shopping for a computer, focus on the basic components. The CPU or Central Processing Unit is the controller of the system. It should have at least 2 megabytes of memory. It receives all incoming data and instruction and directs the information to the disk, screen or printer. The hard disk should have a minimum of 40 megabytes of storage as it will store all of your information. The quality of the color monitor is important as you and your student will spend many hours reading from it. The VGA monitor is the only color monitor that is really acceptable for text. Make sure the keyboard feels comfortable to you and check the quality and speed of the printer.

Upgrading Your Computer

If you already own a computer that does not come up to the basic standards recommended (see Appendix A), it may be possible for you to upgrade your existing system rather than buying a new one. However, it is often a close call between upgrading and getting a new system. The following are basic upgrade steps. You will need to talk to a computer technician to tell you how feasible and economical they are for the system you are currently running.

1. Upgrade Motherboard: If you have an old PC that is extremely slow, you can upgrade the motherboard to a 286 or 386. Often the power supply and hard disks in the older systems are not worth saving, making upgrading questionable.

2. Add Memory: If you don't have at least 640 k of memory, you must add memory to at least that level, but preferably to 2 megabytes.

3. Upgrade Monitor: To run many of the education programs properly, you will need a color graphics card and the corresponding monitor. I strongly recommend VGA. If buying a used one, EGA is acceptable but do not buy a CGA monitor.

4. Keyboard: If you are using the old basic keyboard, you will appreciate a full 101 keys and superior arrow and enter keys. The feel of the keyboard is important.

5. Mouse: Highly recommended. It takes a little time to get used to it but it will speed up many different programs.

6. Printer: If you have a non-graphics or daisy wheel printer you should definitely upgrade. (See printer recommendations for systems A and B.) Inkjet and laser printers are the main choices today.

Where should Your Computer Live ?

An element of providing a good environment is setting up a quiet workplace with a desk and a comfortable chair. If a room is equipped with a stereo, television and phone, sending a child there to do homework may be tantamount to sending a cat to study peaceful coexistence in the dog house.

It is material that the workplace for the student be easily accessible and neat. Space is obviously an important criteria. Students need room to layout papers and books. Easy access to the computer is critical. If using the system requires moving a table and chairs, the students's use of the PC will go down directly in proportion to the difficulty of setting it up. If the system is put on a kitchen counter that barely has room, work will be difficult and the computer will not be properly utilized.

A computer desk is useful as it gives plenty of room for everything. I recommend buying one. There are many computer desks available in a variety of price ranges that make working with a PC a much more pleasurable experience.

You will also need an electrical outlet with enough capacity to handle the equipment. A surge protector, (a device that will prevent a sudden rush of current from damaging your computer or data,) is also a very worthwhile investment. **DO NOT** plug your computer into the same line as a major appliance. Although computers are not as sensitive to heat as they once were, it is still a good idea to have adequate ventilation. The general rule is that if you are comfortable, your PC will be comfortable.

Final Note

It is important to remember that the recommendations in this chapter are only guidelines for purchasing a PC. The market is changing so quickly that today's best choices may not be the best six months from now. It is important to recognize that what drives the computer is software. A knowledgeable and responsible salesperson will help guide you in your hardware choice based on the software you are going to use.

Many companies will give you a money back guarantee. If you make your purchase with the guidelines given here, it should not be necessary to use that guarantee. (But fill out all the paperwork anyway.)

(For Details on types of computer systems see Appendix A:)

Chapter 5

Introduction to Educational Software

For the Parent and Student

In this chapter I will put forth the computer programs that qualify as Educational Software, and will discuss the criteria used in determining if a program meets the requirements of the **Computer Curriculum.** These are the programs that I found exciting when working with my "Computer Chips" at the N.Y.A. They helped to expand the minds of the students in subjects ranging from math, vocabulary and reading to drawing and other creative endeavors. The programs will range in form from games to memory lessons to word drills. These programs are the groundwork for beneficial and challenging educational experience.

There are many different types of educational software. These can be grouped by the age of the student, subject matter, teaching style, or topic. This book, intended for students who are ten to fifteen years old, will focus on the software that is most pertinent for that age group. I will also describe some types of educational programs available and focus on the specific ones used in the **Computer Curriculum.**

The first and oldest type of educational software is called *Drill and Practice.*
At level 1 in the educational hierarchy, this software's primary purpose is to drill on basics such as multiplication or long division and other math related topics. After the program presents a problem, the student types in (inputs) an answer, and the software immediately registers if the answer is correct. The software also drills vocabulary by providing sentences with missing words that the student must supply. This provides a marked contrast to either classroom homework or tests, where incorrect answers are not returned to the student for three or four days. The immediate response mechanism of this software enhances the learning capacity of the

child.

Another type of education software is *tutorial.* Tutorials corresponds to the second level in the educational hierarchy utilizing the results of the drill and practice. This software explains terms and concepts and uses examples to illustrate them. In a vocabulary program, the initial phase of the tutorial will provide a student with the definition of a word and its use in a sentence. The program will then test the student, using a variety of different procedures, such as multiple choice or matching, on the words just seen. If the student misses one or more definitions, the program will display the correct answer. The program will continue to repeat the problems that the student answered incorrectly, will focus on problem areas exhibited by the student and will give him/her extra practice in that arena. Some software programs will track the students scores (percent correct) and print out report cards or certificates of achievement. Many programs will also allow students, through the use of an editor, to add their own problems.

The third level of education is related to **problem-solving.** Problem solving occurs when the student is taught the skill of gathering information. From that information, software can teach deductive and inductive reasoning.

Where in the World is Carmen Sandiego? is an example of problem-solving software. Students use deductive reasoning to recognize clues while they learn geography by chasing criminals around the world.

Computer programs that foster *creativity* are another example of educational software. Creativity, the fourth level of education, is an integral part of building a child's approach to the world and developing self-esteem. There are computer programs that can be used in art, music, design, architecture, writing and publishing. Some examples of this type of program are; ***The New Print Shop,*** a program that  lets students design and produce posters, greeting cards, flyers and other kinds of publications; ***KidPix,*** which will let students exhibit fantastic drawings with very little artistic training; and ***Once Upon a Time,*** which can produce very complex illustrated stories. ***Word processing*** programs can be used to write illustrated reports, make use of creative forms of lettering and produce documents of near professional quality. Because creativity can be different for each individual, it is very difficult to measure.

General software packages can have educational value. Although Word Processing was designed for business or professional use, students can use it to write reports, stories, or essays. In addition there are specialized programs available for geometry, science, ecology, sociology and many other subjects. There are also programs to help students prepare for the PSAT and SAT examinations. We will describe these programs in ***Chapter 15: Other Software.***

Criteria for Good Educational Software

Based on my evaluation of educational software packages, my work with a wide range of children, and my research into the best methods of teaching/learning, I have defined the following criteria for selecting good software packages:

The program should:

- expand the student's horizon.

- provide immediate feedback so students can correct mistakes at once.

- be self-motivating and enjoyable to the student.

- have multiple facets so problems can be approached in different ways.

- have multiple levels of difficulty.

- have record keeping ability to track the student's progress.

- give students an opportunity to create their own lessons, allowing them to input specific subjects they are studying in school.

Although my dream of the perfect educational software package has not yet been realized those that I have chosen meet at least a few of the above criteria.

Basic Software for the Computer Curriculum

MAVIS BEACON TEACHES TYPING is a program that takes students through all of the steps necessary to become a good typist. The program has the ability to pinpoint the letters that give students the most difficulty and to devise special exercises for them. It keeps track of progress and has the capability of working with typing ability of all levels .

MATH BLASTER PLUS is a program that develops problem solving strategies and patterns. It starts with addition and subtraction, moves on to multiplication and division and then progresses to working with fractions. From there it advances to decimals, percentages and conversions between them. All of this is done in a graphic game form that students find interesting and motivating as well as enjoyable.

MATH BLASTER MYSTERY is a program that develops inductive and deductive reasoning skills. It teaches problem solving strategies. Students who develop problem-solving skills will be more successful in all aspects of life than those who have not developed these skills. Although a math program, many of the skills *Math Blaster Mystery* develops are much broader than pure mathematical applications. Students identify relevant and irrelevant information, guess and check to close in on an answer and analyze ambiguous situations.

ALGE-BLASTER PLUS! covers the materials in both the first and second semesters of algebra. Rational numbers, combining monomials and polynomials, working with linear equations and integers, fractions and decimals are covered. It also explains and develops problems in the basics of graphing and finding points on a graph and the related slope. This is a learning program with a step-by-step interactive tutorial that assists the student.

WORD ATTACK PLUS! teaches new words and definitions in a game format that builds vocabulary skills essential to reading and writing. The program works with definitions, using words in sentences and spelling them correctly. The game aspect, along with score keeping, motivates the students and gets them excited about learning.

OREGON TRAIL lets students relive the exciting days of pioneers and covered wagons. The program asks students to choose a profession: banker, farmer, storekeeper or carpenter. Depending on what profession they choose, the program gives players an amount of money to buy supplies. It helps them decide what supplies to buy and teaches money management. Once started on the trail students are forced to make choices and listen to people's advice. If they make good choices, they will reach Oregon. Otherwise, they will die along the trail. This program teaches students to learn from others, trade, and generally simulates a real trip to Oregon.

MICROSOFT WORKS is a word processing program which replaces the typewriter. It lets students make corrections easily, and permits moving sections of text around to improve the flow of a document. It also checks spelling, pointing out errors and giving replacement choices with the correct spelling. Finally, it prints a document that is easy for teachers to read. Because of its ease of use and the ability to quickly correct and rewrite, the average student is apt to write a longer and more meaningful paper using a word processing program.

WHERE IN THE WORLD IS CARMEN SANDIEGO? lets student sleuths track down Carmen and her henchmen. Solving cases is exciting but far from easy. This program challenges both the logical and geographical ability of students. They must learn to recognize cryptic bits of information, take diligent notes and look up reference data in the world almanac. They must make decisions based upon a time frame to permit them to capture Carmen Sandiego's henchman before it's too late. This is a decision game with a lot of basic geographical facts thrown in. Thousands of permutations and hundreds of clues force the player to learn about the world and its history. Fun for the individual, it can also be played by several students working together. In the process, the students learn the research skills that can separate a successful pupil from a struggling student.

ONCE UPON A TIME takes certain basic elements of a picture such as a backdrop of a main street, and permits the student to add pictures of cars, a church, a gas station and other landmarks. Then the student writes a story based on the picture. This is a program that stimulates imagination while it educates. It also builds vocabulary along with spelling skills and story line development.

THE NEW PRINT SHOP is a productivity tool, like paper and pencil or a canvas and a paint brush. The student can use it to create announcements, banners, and award certificates. This program fosters social and interpersonal skills. Students make greeting cards for friends and family to help commemorate special occasions. It opens up the mind of the student to new possibilities in the use of the computer.

Summary

Each of these programs will be discussed in detail and you will be given all the steps for installing and using them. This chapter was a sneak preview of what we will be working on and the learning paths we will be following.

Chapter 6

Working with Your Computer

For Parents and Students

Welcome to the world of computers. Whether you are a parent, teacher or student, there is something about the power of computers that will captivate you. They are fun and exciting and therefore extremely compatible with children. Computers make ideal teaching tools.

Divided into three separate sections, this chapter provides standard definitions of computer terms, explains basic computer commands and functions and uses a story to illustrate various commands and how the functions work.

While computer terminology may sound complicated, it is relatively simple. There are about 25 words that you need to know to make full use of computers. After you read the definitions of terms, you will be ready to study the rest of this chapter and find out how these commands and functions are used in working with computers.

Glossary of Computer terms

computer: An electronic machine that will respond to a set of instructions, such as a command to add two numbers. A computer can execute a series of these instructions that have been prerecorded in a program.

hardware: Refers to objects that you can actually touch such as disk drives, keyboards, screens, printers and all the electronic and mechanical gear inside the computer box.

monitor: A screen that displays letters, numbers and pictures. It comes in monochrome (basically black and white although most often light green on dark green) or full color similar to a color television.

keyboard: Similar to a typewriter keyboard except that it has additional keys for computer functions such as delete and insert.

CPU: Central Processing Units, the brains of the computer where most calculations take place.

cursor: A small marker, usually a blinking line, box or arrow, which shows where you are on the monitor screen. The cursor indicates where the next letter or symbol will appear on the screen as you type. You can move the cursor using a mouse or directional arrow keys on the keyboard.

memory: (RAM) Random Access Memory. A temporary electronic storage space the computer needs to hold programs and data.

peripherals: Any external device attached to a computer. Peripherals include printers, disk drives, keyboards, monitors, and mice.

floppy disk: A square object with magnetic material on it that stores information in much the same way that an audio cassette tape records sounds. There are two types of floppy disks, the 5 1/4 inch and the 3 1/2 inch. These come in double density (DD) and high density (HD). High density disks can store more data than double density disks.

hard disk: A sealed disk drive usually inside the computer. It can store lots of information. Most hard disk drives can store the equivalent of more than 5,000 typed pages.

printer: A device that prints text or illustrations on paper. The major types of printers are dot-matrix, ink-jet and laser.

mouse: A hand-held device that rolls on the desk or a pad allowing you to move your cursor around the screen very quickly. Many of the newest programs require a mouse.

operating system: The most important program that runs on a computer. Every computer must have an operating system. The operating system performs basic tasks such as recognizing what you are typing on the keyboard, reproducing your typed instructions on the monitor's screen, keeping track of files you create and controlling devices such as disk drives and printers.

MS-DOS: An operating system that runs on all IBM compatible computers. It is basically a single user, single task operating system. That means it runs one job or program at a time.

software: (program) Software consists of sets of instructions or programs stored magnetically on floppy or hard disks. The software program tells the computer what to do and turns it into a teaching machine, a word processor, or a creative tool.

compatibility: The ability of software to run with any specific computer. All software is not compatible with all computers. For example, a word processing program designed for an Apple Macintosh will not work on an IBM PC because Apple and IBM computers are not compatible.

menu: A list of programs which usually appears on your screen when you first turn on your computer. The list includes the programs currently available on that computer. There are also menus within certain programs. On some standard menus, a letter or numbers is assigned to each program. For example:

> A. Word Processing
> B. Personal Finance
> C. Math Game.

When you press A, your computer will automatically be given the command to bring the program into memory so that it is ready to use the word processing program. Menus are very helpful in that they give you a simple one-step --one key -- command to start a program. This saves you from having to type a series of complex DOS commands to start word processing or an educational game. Other common menus allow you to simply move a lightbar to the program you wish to use and then press the < Enter > key on the keyboard or click the button on your mouse.

computer chip: A small piece of semiconducting material usually silicon on which an integrated circuit is embedded. Chips inside your computer make up the brains of the operation.

Computer Curriculum: The use of computers to enhance the learning process. What this book is all about.

windows: A menu type program that replaces most DOS commands with easy-to-use graphic interfaces.

Computer Graphics: A program that gives the computer the ability to display and manipulate pictures.

About the computer

Your computer is made up of many different electronic and mechanical parts generally referred to as *hardware*. The computer operates by following a pre-recorded set of instructions called *software*. To use your computer, you put a disk (*software*) in your computer (*hardware*) and give the computer (*operating system* (**DOS**)) a command to follow the instructions on the disk (*programs*). Word processing software, for example, contains sets of instructions which permit you to use the computer to type a letter, check its spelling, then send the final draft to your *printer* where it is printed out. Hardware and software work together in this way to help your children learn new concepts, do their homework and study quickly and efficiently.

What is hardware

Hardware is the part of your computer that you see and touch. A basic computer hardware system is made up of a *monitor*, a *keyboard,* and the large metal box which contains the chips and other electronic and mechanical gear which make up the computer itself. The computer includes a *floppy disk drive*, a *hard disk drive*, the **CPU** (Central Processing Unit or brains of the computer) and a video card. The video card provides the color graphics including the cartoon images popular in educational games. Other hardware items include a *mouse, printer* and a *CD-ROM* (a compact disk device capable of holding large amounts of recorded information such as an entire encyclopedia.)

When you sit down at your computer, the first thing to do is relax. Despite all of the stories you have been hearing, computers don't bite. You don't need to worry about damaging your computer. While it might get damaged if you drop it or spill orange juice onto the keyboard, normal operations like turning it on and off, inserting diskettes, typing or even making mistakes in the commands won't break it.

What makes a Computer unique

One of the most wonderful things about the computer is its flexibility. This book will show how to use a computer to help your children learn new things. That same computer could also be used to track inventory in a retail store, prepare drawings for a stage play, simulate a financial plan for a bank or send electronic mail around the world at tremendous speed. Computers can also do things we haven't even thought of yet. That's why there is an entire industry for programmers who dream up new functions for computers. Because of the imaginative genius of programmers, educational software can help children learn math, vocabulary and other subjects in a way that is easy to understand and entertaining at the same time. Because of the computer's flexibility, programs can be modified to help individual children work in ways that are most comfortable for them.

The Operating System

Nothing frightens and frustrates the beginning PC user more than **DOS,** the Disk Operating System that seems to be a ghost inside the machine. **DOS** requires you to talk to it by typing odd commands such as **DEL, CD** and **MKDIR--** terms only a programmer could love. The concepts behind **DOS** and its arcane language can seem very intimidating for the beginner. **DOS** commands are cryptic and require a major effort to learn. New users are often required to learn **DOS** commands from a manual that is certainly not fun to read. The good news is that even though **DOS** can be very difficult and frustrating, you only need to learn a few of the major commands to set up your computer for educational software. To introduce you to these commands in as painless a manner as possible, we will first **list the commands** you need to learn and then explain them, giving examples of where, when and how they are used.

DOS or C Prompt: C:> If you do not have a menu already loaded into your computer, the first thing you will see when you turn the machine on is **C:>** in the top left corner of the screen. This lets you know that the computer is ready to accept your instructions. The manuals for many of the programs you will use will ask you to type a command or a series of commands at the **C:>** prompt.

NOTE: After you type a **DOS** command, you must press the <Enter> key to make it work. Programmers and computer buffs refer to this as *executing* the command.

Disk Drives: Under DOS, the disk drives for your software are assigned letters: **A, B, C** and in some cases **D**. The usual configuration is as follows:

> **A:** 5 1/4-inch floppy disk drive
> **B:** 3 1/2-inch floppy disk drive
> **C:** hard disk drive

When you start using a new program, the manual for it may instruct you to put the 5 1/4 inch floppy disk into the **A:** drive and copy it to the hard disk or **C:** drive. Although this may sound confusing at first, after you work with your computer for awhile, it will be as simple as ABC.

Changing drives: DOS can only work with the disk of one drive at a time. So if it is working with the **C:** hard drive and you put a floppy disk in the **A:** drive, you have to tell **DOS** to change drives. If you want to change from the hard disk drive **C:** to the floppy drive **A:** in order to load a program:

At the C: > type **A:**   and press < Enter >.

The **A: >** prompt will appear on your screen, which means the computer is ready to work with the instructions on the floppy disk in the **A:** drive.

NOTE: The drive prompts on your screen will look like this **C: >** on your screen but when you type the name of a drive it must be **C:** because colons (:) are used to designate disk drives in DOS commands.

Boot : To load the first piece of software that starts the computer. Often referred to as ``booting the system.'' The software used for booting is usually **DOS**. Most computers purchased today are pre-loaded, (the program has already been installed on the hard disk) with **DOS**.

Preparing Diskettes

Format: New blank diskettes (5 1/4 or 3 1/2) have to be prepared to hold information. Basically, certain DOS instructions need to be recorded on the blank diskette before it can be used. This is called *formatting*.

IMPORTANT: The format command procedure is for blank diskettes only. <u>DO NOT FORMAT</u> disks that come with educational or other programs on them. Those disks are already formatted and contain valuable computer instructions. Formatting will erase any instructions previously recorded on a disk.

Formatting is very simple. To format a new blank disk put it in the A: drive.   At the C: > type:

C: >   **format A:**   press < Enter > .

IMPORTANT: Always be sure to type **A:** or **B:** to format a new blank floppy disk which you have inserted in the **A:** or **B:** drive. Never type **C: > FORMAT** without the **A:** or **B:** designation as it might result in formatting the **C:** drive which would erase **DOS** and all the other programs already on the **C:** drive. Unless you are a computer expert, you never want to format the **C:** drive.

At the end of the format program, the computer will ask you if you want to format another disk in the **A:** drive. If you are formatting several new blank disks, you can remove the newly formatted disk and put another new blank disk into the drive.

You need only format a diskette once.
REMEMBER: Formatting a diskette erases all data on it.

Copying Diskettes

Diskcopy: This command copies the entire contents of one diskette onto another. Use this command to make backup copies of diskettes containing programs or work you have saved such as letters, essays and school papers. It can also be used to share data with another computer user.

In some systems the program will format a disk at the same time it is being copied. There are two forms of the **Diskcopy** command.

C: > diskcopy A: < Enter >

When you type this command, the computer tells you to insert the source disk (the disk containing the information to be copied) in drive **A:** and press any key. The system copies the diskette into the computer's memory. When it is finished, it tells you to insert the target disk (the blank disk) into drive **A:** and press any key. The system then copies the disk.   **Diskcopy** will also format a blank (unformatted) disk.

C: > diskcopy A: B: < Enter >

If you have two drives, use this command to copy the data on a 5 1/4-inch disk in **A:** to a 3-1/2 inch disk in **B**: or vice versa. To copy a 3 1/2-inch disk in **B:** to a 5 1/4-inch disk in **A:** just reverse the command to: diskcopy **B: A:** and the computer will prompt you in a similar manner.

Putting and Storing data in your Computer

The computer you have purchased is probably already loaded with the **DOS** operating system. The next step is to set up the educational programs permanently in the computer. This means copying the programs from their original floppy disks to the **C:** (hard) drive. There are a number of reasons for doing this. First, it is handier to have programs on **C:** because you can start them right after you turn on the computer. Second, most programs run more efficiently from the hard drive, and some programs, including word processing programs, simply can't be run from one floppy disk. Because there are so many instructions in those programs they need the space that is available on the **C:** drive.

Before loading programs, you need to set up **Directories** to organize your **Files.**

Some terms you'll need to know in working with directories:

Root Directory: The top directory in a file system. In most systems, **C:** is the root directory.

Directories: A file used to organize other files. It can be pictured as a file cabinet.

Sub Directory:
If Directory **C:** holds another directory ED then ED is a sub directory of **C:** and **C:** is the parent of ED.

Files: A collection of data or information. It can be pictured as a file folder.

\ **(backslash)** The \ is an extremely important part of the syntax of typing commands that will take you to a certain level of your directory. The \ separates each directory, sub-directory and file.

To get to the *Newdata* sub directory file starting from the **C:>** prompt, you would use the backslash \ to separate each directory and sub directory as follows:

C:> CD\algebra\newdata

With the \ (backslash), **DOS** knows which path to follow to the file you want.

Copy: This command will copy files from one drive to another or from one directory to another.

C:> copy A:\letter C:\letter

This copies the file LETTER from drive **A:** to drive **C:** It does not remove it from drive **A:**

Making Directories

Imagine walking into a library that is filled with thousands of books which have never been catalogued. These books are spread all over the rooms. Even though you know that the books you are looking for exist in that library, you know that you have no chance to locate them.

Your hard disk is like a library. It can hold an immense amount of information but, to take control, you need to organize it. The first move towards organization is to determine how things are to be organized. We create a cabinet for our books, a special shelf for all books on education. This is the same as creating a directory for our hard disk. In order to store information away we must create or make directories.

MKDIR or **MD:** Typing the command and a directory name will create the sub-directory of that name.

To do this at the C:> type:

C: > **mkdir ed**   press < Enter >

This will create the directory ED. (You can also use the short form of the **MKDIR** command, which is **MD**).

REMEMBER: The name of any directory or sub-directory is limited to 8 characters with no spaces allowed.

When you create a directory, the computer sets up two sub directories, these are called dot directories. One has a single dot (.) and the second has a double dot (..). These directories are reference files for **DOS.** The single dot describes the current directory and the double dot describes the next directory up in the tree structure.

Once you have created your directory you need to be able to move back and forth from directory to directory. To do that you use the change directory command, **CHDIR** or **CD**.

Change Directories CHDIR or **CD** command to change directories.

To change from the **C:** root directory to you MATH sub directory, at the C: > prompt you type:

C: > **cd\MATH** < Enter >

This changes the root directory **C:** to the ED directory. The screen now reads:

C:MATH>

You are now in the **MATH** sub-directory and can work with any program or file in it.

You can also copy files into a directory. If, for example, you have a file on a floppy diskette in drive **A:** and you want to copy it to the ED directory on the **C:** hard disk, you would type:

C: > **copy A:letter C:/ed**

NOTE: You leave a space between the command COPY and the disk drive with the file (**A:LETTER**) and another space between the filename (LETTER) and the drive (**C:**) it is being copied to.

The command above will copy the file LETTER from the diskette in drive A: to the ED directory on the **C:** drive.

Listing Directories

Once you have a number of files in a directory, you may want to see a list of them to find out exactly what is there. The easiest way is to enter the directory using the **DIR** command.

At the C: > type dir <Enter>

This will list the directory for you. It will look like this:

```
WINHELP   HLP    41756    07-15-92  6:08
ALGEBRA   BMP    32234    06-12-91  5:15
MATH            <DIR>         07-15-92  4:30
```

The first word is the file name, the next three letters are the file extension usually indicating what type of file it is. The numbers tell how many bytes of disk space the program takes and the date and time is when the program was loaded.
<DIR> appearing after a file name signifies a directory containing additional files.

If the directory is longer than one page, you may want to use the **DIR/P** command instead of the **DIR** command. This will list the directories one page at a time. If you are in one directory and want to list another directory, you must type the name of the directory you want to list. For example:

At the C: > type dir C:\math

This will list the files in the math directory.

Renaming files REN

As you create more data files, you may reach a point where you want to rename some of them. When you begin writing letters with your word processing program, you may be content to name them: LETTER, LETTER-1, LETTER-2 etc. As you create more files you might want to include a person's name in the file name. To do this, you use the **REN** command to rename the file. Using the three-character dot extension to the eight character filename, you might want to indicate all letters with .LTR using the person's first, last name or initials as the file name. Then your letter to Anne Compton might be named ANNE.LTR or you might use COMPTON or the initials AC.

To rename LETTER to ANNE.LTR, you would type the following command:

C: > **ren letter anne.ltr** < Enter >

REMEMBER: You have eight characters for the initial filename and three more after the (.) dot extension for a total of eleven. If you write to Anne often and want to save each letter on your disk, you may want to number them like this:

ANNE-01.LTR
ANNE-02.LTR
ANNE-03.LTR

Erasing files ERASE or DEL

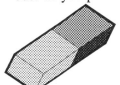

Just as you periodically need to clean out the old files in a filing cabinet, it is a good idea to clean out your computer directories. Do this by deleting files that are no longer needed. For example, after three months, you may no longer need to keep your letter to Anne. To erase the file called ANNE.LTR, move to the directory ANNE.LTR is in and type:

C: > **erase anne.ltr** < Enter >   or   C: > **del anne.ltr** < Enter >

This will erase the ANNE.LTR file.

Erasing with Wild Cards * and ?

The * and ? are symbols known as wild cards. They can be used to represent any character in directory filenames or extensions. They work with a wide variety of DOS commands and can be real time savers. Wild cards are most frequently used with **DIR, COPY** and **DEL (ERASE)**.

The **?** represents a single character. If you wanted to copy all files that started with ANNE, you would type ANNE???? where the **?** represents any letter or number. Remember, file names have up to eight characters followed by optional three-character extension. Thus the full command for copying all your letters to Anne would be ANNE????.LTR, which would give you all the letters starting with ANNE in a particular directory.

Where the **?** represents a single character, the * represents multiple characters. In our example of the letters to Anne, copying all the letters to her could be simplified by using * to designate ANNE*.LTR. The * can also be used to represent the entire file name such as *.LTR if you wanted to copy all your .LTR files regardless of filename. The * can also be used for the dot extension(.). If you had letters to Anne with the extension .LTR and memos to Anne with the extension .MEM you could select them all for copying or deleting by typing ANNE*.* in the command.

Removing Directories RD

As part of your periodic housecleaning of files, you may find directories that are no longer needed. While taking a course in psychology, you may have set up a directory called **psych** for all your term papers and notes. After the course is completed, you may find you no longer use or need the **psych** directory. Just as files can be deleted, directories can be removed.

To remove a directory, first delete (**DEL**) all of the files in it, either by using wild cards or one by one. Once all files have been deleted, you can remove the directory. To do this you must go to the root directory (usually C: >)and type:

C: > rd psych < Enter >

If the **psych** directory is empty this will remove it. If the directory is not empty, this error message will come on the screen:

INVALID PATH OR DIRECTORY NOT EMPTY

This same error message will come up if you try to remove the directory while you are in it. After this message you will be returned to the **C: >** prompt.

Backing up data

Backup helps protect valuable programs and data files on the **C:** drive by copying them from the hard disk to one or more floppies. The hard disk will usually require several floppy disks for backup. The more data on your hard disk, the more floppies required to back it up. Label and number the floppies to keep track of them. The backup program will prompt you when it is time to change disks. To begin backing up the hard disk :

At the C: > type backup press < Enter >

The program will prompt you as to what to do.

Restore is used in the event that the hard disk becomes unusable. This is commonly called a hard disk crash. **Restore** will take the backup data from the floppies and restore it on the hard disk.

CHECKDISK: This command will show how many floppy disks are needed to back up your system.

The Keyboard and special keys

Keyboard: A set of typewriter keys that enable you to enter data into your computer. In addition to the regular typewriter keys on a computer keyboard, there are a number of special computer keys:

Toggle keys: Toggle keys are like switches; when you press them once, they turn on a certain computer function -- press them again, they turn it off. For example, when you press the <Ins> (insert) key it turns on Typeover. (This is not true for all programs or systems). Typeover means that when you move the cursor to a point and start typing, it will type over the characters that are already there. This command will show up on the screen. When you press the <Ins> key again, it turns off Typeover and goes back to the insert mode. When you move the cursor to a certain point and type, it will insert the letters without typing over the existing characters.

Arrow keys: The arrow keys enable you to move the cursor up and down or sideways without affecting the text. Arrow keys allow you to move wherever you want to go on the screen.

<Backspace> The backspace key (a backwards arrow) moves you back one space at a time and in most programs erases the characters on the screen as it goes.

<Caps Lock> This key locks the shift function on so you can type in all capitals. It does not affect the numeric or punctuation keys.

<Esc> Short for Escape. The escape key can have many different functions. It is often used to go back to the previous step in a program., or to send special functions to printers.

<CTRL> The control key is used with other keys to produce control commands such as Quit Program. Its use depends upon which program (software) is running.

For the control key to function, you must hold it down while pressing another key designated in the program to perform a certain function. For example, if the manual for a software program tells you to press <CTRL> Y to exit the program, you would hold down the <Ctrl> key while pressing the Y key. Pressing the <Ctrl> key, then releasing it and pressing the Y key will NOT work. The two keys must be held down simultaneously.

<ALT> The alternate or <Alt> key functions in the same way as the control key. Again, it depends on the program. In some programs for example, holding down the <ALT> key and X key simultaneously will allow you to exit the program. The <CTRL> and <ALT> keys allow the existing keys on the keyboard to perform additional functions. For example, when typing in a word processing program, pressing the X key by itself simply produces the letter X in a word like exit. But <CTRL> X may allow you to exit the program and <ALT> X may produce a special symbol such as a bullet or star. Thus the X key can have three functions rather than one.

<Del> The delete key erases the character at the cursor. Used in conjunction with other keys it can delete lines or pages.

<Enter>: The <Enter> key, is the equivalent of the old carriage return key on a typewriter. (You may sometimes find older programs which tell you to press the Return key. Don't be confused, it's the same as the Enter key.) The <Enter> key is one of the most frequently used on the keyboard. Whenever you have finished a command or want to go on to the next section, <Enter> is the key you press.

Function Keys: Function keys are the ones marked F1 through F10 (some keyboards have 12). These keys perform different functions depending on the program you are running. Most current programs use <F1> as the help key, some use <F7> as the exit key, and combinations such as <ALT> <F1> for checking spelling or other functions. (Remember to hold down the <ALT> or <CTRL> key and the function key at the same time.) Most programs come with a template (a type of map) which is put above the function keys to show how they operate in that particular program.

<Tab> The tab key works very much as it does on a typewriter. The standard tab setting is five spaces but you can set them any way you want. The tab key is useful for setting up forms and columns. Computers also have reverse tabs which can be used by holding down shift and hitting the tab key to move one tab back. Some programs also use the tab key to move from one part of a form to the next. After filling in the name of a person in a data base program, you would press the tab key to go to the space for the street address.

<Shift> Used to create capital letters or the symbols above the numbers, the shift key is also used in conjunction with the function keys to perform certain functions. For example, <Shift> <F7> might be the print command in word processing.

<Home> In many programs this key or some combination of this key with another key will bring you to the top (beginning) of the page.

<PgDn> In many programs pressing this key will move the document one page down. This does not mean one screen but actually the equivalent of a printed page.

<PgUp> This key will move the document one page up. It also is used to send special codes to a printer or disk drive and to step back (return to the previous command) in certain programs. It is often used to cancel the previous command.

<End> The <End> key usually moves the cursor to the end of the line. In conjunction with other keys, it can perform other functions, such as delete to end of line, or delete to end of page, etc.

<Ins> As discussed earlier, <Ins> is a toggle key that can be used either to insert characters into a word or if toggled on to type over any characters on the screen.

<Num Lock> This key is used to lock the ten-key pad on the keyboard so that it can be used of numbers only. This is most often used in math and accounting programs.

<Ctrl-Alt-Del> Holding down the <CTRL> <ALT> and <Del> keys at the same time will cause the system to re-boot or start over. Some programs ask you to do this after you install them. In the event that the computer freezes up on you and you cannot get it to react to the <ESC> key or any other commands, you may have to re-boot to get the computer working again. At that point you would lose all unsaved data.

Making use of the Major Keys

This is a story to help illustrate the use of some of the major keys:

In writing a letter, Jane noticed that she had misspelled the word conjunction four lines back. She had spelled it conjunttion. She used her arrow keys to move up four lines and over until the cursor was at the first t in conjunttion. She used her delete <Del> key to remove the unwanted t. Then, making certain that the <Ins> key was on, so she was in insert mode, she typed the c needed to correct the spelling mistake. Next, she decided that there might be other spelling errors so she wanted to use the spelling checker in the word processing program. She had forgotten what keys she needed to press to start the spelling checker so she pressed <F1> (the help key in that program) and learned that spell check could be activated by pressing <ALT> <F2>. She held down the <ALT> key and pressed <F2>. The spell check was activated.

When she wanted to quit the spell check program, she hit <ESC> which brought her back to the document. Jane decided that the next paragraph should be in all capital letters so she pressed the <Caps Lock> key to keep the caps on for that paragraph. When she finished, she pressed the <Caps Lock> key again to return the keyboard to normal function. She wanted the next sentence underlined so she pressed <ALT> <F6> and the sentence was underlined. After she finished she wanted to print the document so she held down <Alt> and pressed <F7> and the document printed. When she was through with the document she pushed <F10>. This saved her work and took her out of the program back to the main menu.

The function keys mentioned in this program are specific to that program and the word processing program you will be using might use different keys.

Chapter Summary

This chapter has introduced you to the terminology of the computer, the operating system, its most important functions and the keyboard with its special keys. You have learned about the major keys on the keyboard and how they are used to execute computer commands. As you and your student load and run the educational programs, with the help of this book, you will become familiar and comfortable with their various functions.

Chapter 7

The Curriculum

For the Parent

The **Computer curriculum** presented in this book is designed to balance *learning to use* the computer with *using* the computer as a tool for learning. We are not pushing students into the world of computers, but toward a world that is using computers. To prepare students for this world we must teach them on a computer system that is easy to use, provide a working environment that is conducive to utilizing the computer and develop a personalized curriculum at their level where progress can be measured. This system should be integrated into a personalized reward system that will keep the student motivated.

Because we want students to progress at their own learning capacity the following curriculum offers not an exact study plan, but guidelines to develop a personalized plan for each student. You can take the lesson plan and tailor it to fit each student's needs. A student who is proficient in math, could spend time on *Word Attack*, spelling and writing; one who is a good writer and reader with an excellent vocabulary but who has little comprehension of percentages, should spend time on programs such as *Math Blaster* or *Algebra.*

Preparing a three-month Plan

Because planning is a very important function in any project, preparing a three month written plan with specific goals is advantageous for this program. This plan helps to focus on problem areas and establish goals for the student. The goals may be as basic as learning the multiplication tables and typing 10 words per minute, or more demanding, like writing a four page report on "global warming". A reward for completing the first three months and achieving individual goals will help motivate the student. Allowing students to participate in choosing their own rewards can create an even stronger motivation.

The initial curriculum includes typing, vocabulary, math and a decision-making game. Each of these programs has a definite function in the education of a child. In typing, vocabulary and math it is easy to measure progress. The effect of the decision-making game cannot be ascertained as quantitatively as the others, but you'll begin to notice greater clarity in the students' thinking as they work through everyday problems. Experience in decision making and problem solving is a valuable lesson for any student.

The amount of time each student spends on the curriculum will vary. The minimum amount, to achieve a significant level of progress, is two hours per week for a three month period. In my experience, once students get started and feel comfortable with the computer, they begin to ask to spend more time on it. To allow this to happen within the structure of this lesson plan, I have set up a flexible hourly curriculum broken down into 30-minute segments. This allows students to progress at their own individual pace. These 30 minute segments should be used only as a guideline. Each student's interest and progress should be gauged to decide the best use of time.

In Chapter 15, ***Other Software that will Help Educate*** I recommend other software that can be used in this program. If you as a parent/teacher feel that your student is spending enough time on the regular programs and has a good understanding of the work, these supplemental program can be used.

Developing the Starting Point

We have provided a set of tests to decide the starting level for each student (See Appendix B). The tests serve two functions. First, they decide the level at which your student can begin working in the math program *(Math Blaster Plus)* and vocabulary program*(Word Attack Plus)*. Second, they establish a base against which to record progress. Appendix B contains forms on which the progress of each student can be recorded. Showing progress and giving encouragement and rewards for performance is an important part of this curriculum that helps keep students interested and motivated.

Vocabulary Testing

The vocabulary test consists of 48 words with multiple-choice matching questions. The time allotted for the test is 25 minutes. Correct the test when the student has completed it. The student's starting point would be one level below the point where two or more answers were incorrect. For example, a student who misses two words in level five should start at level four. If only one mistake is made at a given level, it's a judgment call. In general, it is better to start at a lower level and let the student move up quickly rather than start at too difficult a level , which could lead to frustration. This is especially true if it is the first time the student has used a computer for an extensive period. Students should feel comfortable with the computer experience. Initial success goes a long way toward making the curriculum enjoyable.

Math Testing

The math test consists of 25 problems. The level corresponding to the computer program is shown on the test sheet. In an abbreviated test of this type it is difficult to be certain of the level a student has really attained. If there is any doubt, start at the lower level. The student will become familiar with the computer and the program while building to a proper level.

The testing is designed to suggest starting levels for vocabulary and mathematics. It is only an indicator and is intended to be used as a guideline in the **Computer Curriculum.**

Writing

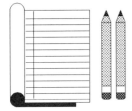 Each student should spend thirty minutes, with pen and paper, writing about a familiar subject; a hobby, a sport, a pet -- or a topic such as *What I want to do on my next vacation.* Keep the essay on file. Six months from now, ask the student to spend 30 minutes writing a similar essay on another topic using the computer's word processing program. A comparison of the two essays will show the student's progress. You will be delighted to see the difference.

After you have completed the proscribed tests and recorded the recommended level for starting the vocabulary and math programs, you are ready to start the **Computer Curriculum.**

The 30-minute Schedule

The amount of time a student should devote to each section can vary. An amount of time should be designated for each lesson, but there should be flexibility in this process. It is important to be goal oriented, i.e. completing a section rather than putting a lot of emphasis on the amount of time spent on the section. Research into education tells us that classes are most successful when they don't have specific time limits. If students become absorbed in a program, it is best not to cut them off just to adhere to a schedule. The lesson plans are guidelines. They are not inflexible rules.

Class 1: Introduction to the Computer: This class will help your student learn some basic computer concepts as outlined in the beginning sections of this book. Begin with the program *Mavis Beacon Teaches Typing* as the first lesson. You can progressively introduce other subjects as suggested by this schedule.

	Typing	Word Attack	Math Blaster	Oregon Trail
Class 2:	x	x		
Class 3:	x	x		
Class 4:	x		x	
Class 5:	x	x		
Class 6:	x		x	
Class 7:	x	x		
Class 8:	x		x	
Class 9:	x	x		x
Class 10:	x		x	x

This is an example of how the class/play schedule could work for the first three months. If students can do all the levels in *Math Blaster*, move them on to a more difficult program such as *Algeblaster*. If they becomes bored with *Oregon Trail* then introduce them to *Carmen Sandiego.*

The Second Level

During the second group of classes **Microsoft Works** is used to inaugurate students on a writing program which will supplement or alternate with their typing. When students first start writing it may be difficult for them to think of subjects. As the curriculum proceeds generating topics will become easier. At this point in time students should be encouraged to accomplish some of their homework on the computer. Essays, book reports and science projects are a few of the items that could easily be produced on the computer.

Some Suggested Topics for Essay

Listed below are some topics for student essays.

Something I did that made my mother happy.

My favorite relative.

My favorite television program.

The silliest thing I ever bought.

My favorite subject in school
.

When using these topics try to get students involved in creating some of their own themes.

This section also introduces a new program called, ***Where in the World is Carmen Sandiego?*** and a graphic program called ***The New Print Shop.***

The classes:

Class 1: Teaches the fundamentals of word processing so students can start their writing careers. (See the section on *Microsoft Works*) It will probably take two sessions for students to become familiar with the program.

At this time your student is ready to be introduced to that master criminal, *Carmen Sandiego* and her band of vile henchmen. It is helpful to show students how to use reference books, such as the almanac, to do the some of the basic research required for capturing *Carmen*.

Class 2: Additional training on Word processing.
Capture a criminal in *Carmen Sandiego*.

Setting Up an Individualized Lesson Plan

At this point in the curriculum it becomes more difficult to lay out a standard lesson plan that will apply to all students. The skill levels, interests and areas needing improvement will vary for each student. One of the most valuable aspects of the **Computer Curriculum** is that it allows for individualized instruction. With that in mind, you can set up a weekly lesson plan for your students based on their needs and interests. Follow the broad outlines given in this chapter and modify them to meet the needs of your students.

Three Month Milestone

At the end of three months students should be re-tested to see how they are progressing. Weekly record keeping and contacts with your children will show you the progress they have achieved. By doing a three-month test, you'll have data showing the change in the student's level in vocabulary and math.

Six Month Milestone

At this point you should repeat the testing procedure using the same methods as you did at the end of three months. This is the last time you will use the standard tests because, after this, your record keeping and the student's growing proficiency in reading and writing will show the real progress being made.

Writing After Six Months

Have students sit at the computer and write an essay using the same topic and amount of time as the initial essay written six months ago. You are almost certain to see a tremendous difference in both style and content. This is currently the student's way of communicating with teachers. In the future this method will be employed to apply for jobs, send letters to friends, and communicate with business associates. Your children have started on a road that will make a significant difference in their futures.

Building Strengths

Throughout the Computer Curriculum, emphasize those areas where students have the greatest weakness. They will want to work with programs where they are the strongest and say that the other programs are *too difficult* or *no fun*. At this juncture review the goals of this curriculum to make certain that the student is working on those areas that need to be strengthened most.

Setting Up Record keeping

In Appendix B, you will find record keeping forms for *Mavis Beacon Teaches Typing, Word Attack Plus and Math Blaster plus.* They should be copied onto regular paper and put in a notebook or file. Details on how to keep records are in **Appendix C.**

Mavis Beacon Teaches Typing

The key to good typing is speed and accuracy. Fortunately accuracy today is not as important as in the past. With word processing and spell checking, typos are corrected quickly and easily.

In Appendix B there is a graph to show student progress. As students reach the breakthrough level, -- we're using 85% but anywhere from 80% to 90% is acceptable -- plot the graph based on level and objects. This gives a good picture (graphic) of progress. It also points out any subject areas where additional practice is needed.

Motivation

Motivation is a crucial part of any educational process. Making studying and learning enjoyable is one way of motivating students. I can cite an example from my own experience that inspired me to develop the Computer Curriculum. I watched a 13-year-old boy practice long division on a computer for 1 1/2 hours and love it! I felt if a computer program could motivate one student, it could be beneficial for many students.

There are other important keys to motivation, which as a parent, you can use to encourage your child. Children watch their parents' behavior, looking for praise and recognition from them. The attitude of the parents towards reading, education, and television establishes the pattern for the child. If you as a parent consider the computer and software programs important, your children will too. If the computer session is constantly rescheduled because of other priorities, the student will no longer consider it very important. It is also important that the session not become a dreaded moment, like taking a hated piano lesson. Set the tone by showing your enthusiasm for the computer and giving praise and recognition to your children.

In recognizing the role of motivation, we must look at some positive and negative motivational factors related to this project. These are factors that apply in school, as well as in the home curriculum.

Motivational factors working against doing the exercises:

"If I don't use the computer I will --"

- have more time for television.
- avoid criticism for not doing well.
- avoid working.

Motivational factors working in favor of doing the exercises:

"If I use the Computer I will--"

- have fun with the computer.
- please my parents and get praised.
- improve my scores (report cards) and show that "I'm making progress."

Praise and Reinforcement

When viewing your child's report, be sure to dwell on the positive. In this program, we always want to recognize the student as an individual, placing the emphasis on progress. Don't compare your student with how another child is doing. Especially avoid negative comparisons.

Here are two examples of the same information being related to a student.

NEGATIVE: *You only got 54% on your verbs. That is really terrible.*

POSITIVE: *You got 54% on your verbs. That is 10% better than last time! We know that next time you will do even better.*

The informational part of the message is the same, but the positive response will help motivate whereas the negative could have a demotivating effect. The child may rationalize by saying *"This is a silly exercise. I don't care how I do any more."*

One of our goals in the **Computer Curriculum** is to help students enhance their self-esteem. This is a building process, which is done by a positive approach to all aspects of the computer curriculum. As they achieve their goals in the program, students will be motivated and their self-esteem will improve.

Setting a goal of typing 15 words per minute can really motivate the student to achieve that target. When the goal is reached, there is a real feeling of accomplishment. It is important to set goals that while not too easy are still achievable. When starting a new program such as *Math Blaster Plus*, it is crucial that the student achieve a goal quickly to avoid thinking *This is too hard, I can't do it*.

Robert E. Slavin in his book *Educational Psychology* states that often in school and at home, children live up to the expectations of their teachers or parents. Thus a child labeled as a troublemaker strives to be one. Children tend to live out the roles that adults, especially parents and teachers, assign to them. That is why it is important to avoid putting labels on children. Avoid being judgmental when talking about a student's problem areas. A child who has been called hopeless at math or spelling may act as if that is the final judgment for those subjects and give up ever trying to improve. Be careful about telling a student that something is too hard for them. Rather, encourage them to try it, even if it is very difficult.

Clear instructions and expectations are very helpful to the student. Be specific. For example, tell the student: *Spend 30 minutes on your vocabulary and finish section 5*. This is much more helpful than if you just say: *Spend some time doing vocabulary*. Being specific also shows a higher level of interest on your part. The idea of clear and specific instructions is helpful in many areas. "*Clean up your room!*" (which may lead to everything being pushed under the bed) is not as helpful an instruction as, "*Pick up everything from the floor and put it neatly in the closet.*" This idea of giving clear instruction is also a learning experience that will serve students well in later life.

When a student completes a section or project specific feedback and praises are important. That is why I emphasize record keeping and the ability to print out *report cards*. This gives the student immediate feedback while giving the parent a tool for measuring progress and directing the student.

Base Score Grading

Measuring progress based upon a students starting level, rather than in absolute terms, is an important idea that can be used with the frequent scores generated within the **Computer Curriculum.** In school students are used to absolute grades of A, B, C, D & F. Some students, because of their background and previous education, have an easy time getting A's and B's, demotivating those who have to work very hard to get C's. Our aim in this program is to recognize growth at every level. Often, a child who improves a grade from a D to a C+ has worked harder and deserves more acclaim than the student who raises a grade from a B to a B+. Most public schools cannot handle this type of grading. It is not in their charter. But, in the individualized curriculum described here, it is easy to establish base level scores giving praise and rewards based on progress rather than on absolute values. The student who starts *Word Attack Plus* on Level 3 and in the first three months of the program goes to level six is performing very well, although not yet reaching his or her true grade level. This concept of progress from the base level is key in the **Computer Curriculum.** Whether your child is considered a poor, average, or gifted student, the **Computer Curriculum** will give him/her a chance to achieve new levels of success and build self-esteem.

Chapter 8

Installing the Programs
and Getting Started

For the Parent

 This chapter explains how to install the educational software for the **Computer Curriculum.** It is divided into two sections.   The first section describes the method for installing programs that teach typing, vocabulary and math. The second section describes the installation of algebra, word processing and decision-making games.

Time to Start

The instructions in this book have helped you to set up your computer, connect the printer and make certain that **DOS** (Disk Operating System) resides on your computer. You have purchased *PC DYNAMIC MENU WORKS,* or a similar
menu program and are now ready to install the basic educational software and setup a menu for the following programs:

•*Mavis Beacon Teaches typing!*

•*Math Blaster Plus*-- basic mathematics.

•*Word Attack Plus* -- vocabulary.

•*Once Upon a Time* -- story writing.

•*Algeblaster* - algebra.

•*Where in The World is Carmen Sandiego?* -- geography and decision making.

•*Microsoft Works* -- writing and word processing.

•*Oregon Trail* -- history, geography, decision making.

•*Math Blaster Mystery*-- problem solving and decision making.

•*The New Print Shop* -- graphics package and desktop publishing.

Preparing the Computer

In this section you will learn how to set up directories and install the programs. Each program has a different section and can be installed separately. I suggest you spend about an hour to install the first four programs, allowing you to start working with your student on the **Computer Curriculum** before all of the programs are installed.

Making Backup Copies of disks

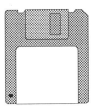 When you purchase computer software on diskettes, it is important to keep your original disks safe. To do this, you should store the originals after creating backup copies that are used to load the programs.

Supplies: To make backup copies of the disks you have purchased you will need:

1. 20 new floppy disks. (5 1/4-inch or 3 1/2-inch)
2. Labels for all the disks.
3. A soft, felt-tipped pen to write on the labels. (Hard pens can scratch the surface of 5 1/4 inch disks - this problem does not exist with 3 1/2 inch disks.)
4. A disk cabinet or box to hold the disks.

Formatting: To format a disk means to prepare it for writing.

FORMAT the disks. Turn on the computer and wait for the C: > prompt. (Type only those letters that are in bold)

1. Insert the blank disk in drive A:

2. At C: > type **FORMAT A:** press < Enter >

At the end of the formatting process **DOS** will ask you if you want to Format another diskette. Follow the instructions to Format ten diskettes so that they are ready for the first phase of installation.

Copying the programs

DISKCOPY: This command copies the entire contents of one disk onto another. It will also format a blank disk at the time it is copying.

1. At C: > type **DISKCOPY A:** press < Enter >

The computer will tell you to insert the source disk *(disk to be copied from)* in drive A: and press any key. The system will copy the diskette to memory and, when this is completed, will tell you to insert the target disk *(your newly formatted disk to be copied to)* in drive A, and to press any key. The system will copy the disk. Use this procedure to make copies of all disks except *Mavis Typing*. Because of special formatting and compression, you cannot make backup copies of *Mavis*.

Label the disks: Write the name of the program you copied onto a label and stick it on the disk. This will become your master disk. Next, protect these disks from being written on or the programs destroyed. For a 5 1/4-inch floppy, use the small black labels that come in the box to cover the write protect notch on the upper right-hand side of the disk. For a 3 1/2-inch floppy, slide the tab as shown in the illustration on the box. Your disks are now write protected.

Creating Directories and Installing Programs

A directory is like a filing cabinet. Most of the programs will create their own directories, but some require the **DOS** Command **MD** to make a directory.

Section I

1. Installing *Mavis Beacon Teaches Typing!*

To install *Mavis Beacon Teaches Typing,* do the following.

1. Go to the C: > prompt.

2. Put Disk 1 in floppy drive A:

3. At C: > type **A:INSTALL** press < Enter >
(Remember -- type only the bold letters.)

Follow the directions on your screen. This screen will tell you when you have completed the installation. The program will create a directory called **Mavis** and store the program inside that directory.

2. *Math Blaster Plus:*

Create a directory for *Math Blaster Plus*

1. Go to the C: > prompt.

2. At C: > type **MD \MATH** press < Enter >

Next set up sub-directories *(folders)* within the math sub-directory. One sub-directory is for special problems students can enter into the system by using the editor function of the program. The second sub-directory is for record keeping, the file that maintains the scores for each student.

To set up these sub-directories:

1. At C: > type **MD \MATH\NEWDATA** press < Enter >

2. At C: > type **MD \MATH\RECORDS** press < Enter >

Once you have set up the sub-directories for math, install *Math Blaster Plus* on our hard disk.

2.A Installing *Math Blaster Plus*

1. At the C: > prompt type **A:** and press < Enter >

2. Put the program disk in the A: drive. *(If you're loading from the B: drive, follow the same procedure but type **B:** For **A:**)*

3. At A: > type **HDINSTALL C:\MATH** press < Enter > >

HDINSTALL is the hard disk installation command. C: is the drive where the program is to be installed and **\MATH** is the directory.[1]

This will install *Math Blaster Plus* on your computer. To continue, follow the program instructions that appear on the screen.

3. *Word Attack Plus*

Create a directory called ``word."

1. At C: > type **MD \WORD** press < Enter >

As with MATH, you'll want to set up two sub-directories of *WORD.* One will be for special vocabulary and the other will be for record-keeping.

To set up these sub-directories, type:

1. C: > **MD \WORD\NEWDATA** press < Enter >

2. C: > **MD \WORD\RECORDS** press < Enter >

You are now ready to install WORD ATTACK PLUS on your hard disk.

3A. Installing *Word Attack Plus*

1. At the C:> prompt type **A:** press <Enter>.

2. Put the program disk in the A: drive.

3. At A:> type **HDINSTALL C:\WORD** press <Enter>

This will install *Word Attack Plus*. Just follow the program instructions as they appear on the screen.

4. *Oregon Trail*

Set up a directory for *OREGON TRAIL*.

1. At the C:> prompt type **MD \OTRAIL** press <Enter>

Once you have set up the *OREGON TRAIL* sub-directories, you're ready to install the program.

Installing *Oregon Trail*

1. Insert the *OREGON TRAIL* disk in drive A:

2. Type **A:** and press <Enter>.

3. At the **A:** prompt type **INSTALL**.
Follow the instructions on the screen. The program will tell you when the installation is complete.

This completes the first section installation. If you want to get started in the program, turn to the **Installing Menu Works** section in this chapter and create your menu for these four programs. If you want to continue installing the other programs, go to the next paragraph.

Section II

5. Algeblaster

Algeblaster and the other programs in this section are loaded with the same basic commands as those in the first section. Just follow the step-by-step directions. If you encounter any problems, check the user manual for the program you are loading.

To set up an algebra sub-directory:

1. At C: > type **MD \ALGEBRA** press < Enter >

After making a sub-directory for *ALGEBLASTER*, set up sub-directories for special problems and record keeping.

2. At C: > type **MD \ALGEBRA\NEWDATA** press < Enter >

3. At C: > type **MD \ALGEBRA\RECORDS** press   < Enter >

5A. Installing *Algeblaster*

Install *Algeblaster* on your hard disk by executing the following procedure.

1. At the C: > prompt type **A:** press < Enter > .

2. Put the program disk in the A: drive.

3. At A: > type **HDINSTALL C:\ALGEBRA** press < Enter >

Follow the program instructions on the screen.

6. Math Blaster Mystery

Set up the usual sub-directories.

    1. At C: > type **MD \MBM** press < Enter >

    2. At C: > type **MD \MBM\NEWDATA** press < Enter >

    3. At C: > type **MD \MBM\RECORDS** press < Enter >

Now you can install the program on your hard disk.

6A. Installing MATH BLASTER MYSTERY

    1. At the C: > prompt type **A:** press < Enter >.

    2. Put the program disk in the A: drive.

    3. At A: > type **HDINSTALL C:\MBM** press < Enter >

Follow the program instructions on the screen.

7. Where in the World is Carmen Sandiego?

    Make a sub-directory for *Where in the World is Carmen Sandiego?*

    1. At the C: > prompt type **MD \WORLD** press < Enter >

7A. Installing *CARMEN*

    1. At the prompt type **A:**

    2. Insert the first disk for CARMEN. Type **Install** and follow the directions on the screen.

Follow the instructions for any of the other Carmen Programs.

8. *Once Upon a Time*

To set up a sub-directory for *Once Upon a Time*:

    1.   At the C: > prompt type **MD \ONCE** press <Enter>

8A. Installing *Once Upon a Time*

    1. Insert the *Once Upon a Time* disk into drive A:

    2. Type **A:** press <Enter>

    3. Type **Install C:\Once** press <Enter>

Follow the directions on the screen.

9. *Microsoft Works* **(WORD PROCESSING)**

Set up a sub-directory for WORD PROCESSING:

    1. At C: > type **MD\WORKS** press <Enter>

    2. At the Dos prompt, type **A:setup** press <Enter>

    3. Follow the directions on the screen.

10. *NEW PRINT SHOP*

Set up a sub-directory for New Print shop.

1. At C: > type **MD\NPS**   press <Enter>

2. Type **Install** press <Enter>

3. Follow the directions on the screen.

Setting Up Your Menu

Using a menu makes it much easier to access the educational programs. *Menu Works* Personal, is a menu program that is easy to install. Once you have set it up with one or two of your programs, adding other programs should be no problem. If *Menu Works* is not available, other menu programs will work as well.

Installing *MENU WORKS* Personal

Installing *MENU WORKS* is similar to installing the individual programs. Put the *MENU WORKS* disk in Drive A:

1. At the C:> prompt type **A:** press <Enter>

2. At the A:> prompt type **install** press <Enter>

3. Read the instructions. Select **Continue** and press <Enter>
   (Select means to move the lightbar to the desired word or sentence)

4. Read and press <Enter>. The program will now install itself.

5. The program will ask if you want to modify your **Autoexec.bat**
   file. This is the startup file that will bring the **Menu** to the screen.
   The answer is Yes. Press <Enter> to continue.

6. Type your name and press <Enter>

7. **DO NOT SCAN THE FILES.** Select **No** and press <Enter>

8. Screen displays, **Menu Creation Completed Successfully**
   Press any key to continue

9. Remove *Menu Works* disk from Drive A: Press any key to continue

10. Select **Reboot** and press <Enter>
The standard Menu will appear on the screen.

Creating Custom Menus

The next step will be to build a custom menu, **ED**, for the Computer Curriculum.

MENU WORKS PE   **PC Dynamics Inc.**

==

F1 Help
F2 Maintenance

Starting Menu

1. Press **F2** for **Maintenance**

MENU WORKS PE   **PC Dynamics Inc.**

Configuration	Security	Menu	Design	Utilities	Tutorials	Exit
		User Menu Maintenance				
		Menu Selection Maintenance				

User Menu Maintenance

2. Use the arrow keys to move cursor to **Menu.**

3. Select **User Menu Maintenance** and press <Enter>.

4. Select **Add** and press <Enter>

5. Type the menu name **ED.**

6. Type the menu heading, **EDUCATION** and press <Enter>
   Press <Enter> again as no pass word is required

7. Select **Accept** and press <Enter>

8. Select **Yes** to add **Ed** to the Main Menu. (Actually Ed becomes the Main Menu.) Press any key to continue

9. Press **Esc** three times to return to an empty menu list

Adding Selections to the Menu

The first program to add to the menu is *Mavis Beacon Teaches Typing!*

1. Press **F2** for **Maintenance**

2. Use arrows to select **Menu**

3. Select **Menu Selection Maintenance** Press <Enter>

4. Type in the name of the **Menu, ED** and press <Enter>

5. Select **Add** and press <Enter>

6. Select **Run Program** and press <Enter>

7. Select **Edit** and press <Enter>

8. For **Selection** type **MAVIS BEACON TYPING**, press <Enter>

9. For **Directory** type **C:\Mavis** press <Enter>

10. For **Execute** type **Mavis** and press <Enter>

11. For **Password** press <Enter>

12. On the bottom of the screen select **Accept** and press <Enter>

This completes the installation of Mavis to the Menu. The other programs are installed in the same way.

At this point you can select **Add** and enter more programs in the **Menu**.

2. Install *Math Blaster Plus*

    1. Select **Add** and press < Enter>

    2. Select **Run Program** and press < Enter>

    3. Select **Edit** and press < Enter>

    4. For **Selection** type **MATH BLASTER PLUS**, press < Enter>

    5. For **Directory** type **C:\Math** press < Enter>

    6. For **Execute** type **Math** and press < Enter>

    7. For **Password** press < Enter>

    8. On the bottom of the screen select **Accept** and press < Enter>

3. Install *Word Attack Plus*

  Repeat procedures 1,2 and 3.

    4. For **Selection** type **WORD ATTACK PLUS,** press < Enter>
    5. For **Directory** type **C:\WAP**
    6. For **Execute** type **WAP** and press < Enter>
    7. For **Password** press < Enter>
    8. On the bottom of the screen select **Accept** and press < Enter>

4. Install *Oregon Trail*

  Repeat procedures 1,2 and 3.

    4. For **Selection** type **OREGON TRAIL** and press < Enter>
    5. For **Directory** type **C:\Otrail**

6. For **Execute** type **Oregon** and press < Enter >
7. For **Password** press < Enter >
8. On the bottom of the screen select **Accept** and press < Enter >

Part one of the installation is now complete. You can now start the **Computer Curriculum** or continue to add the other programs.

Adding More Programs To Your Menu

To add *Algeblaster, Math Blaster Mystery, Carmen Sandiego, Once Upon a Time,* and *Microsoft Works* to the menu you repeat the first steps to get to the maintenance program.

```
    MENU WORKS  PE            PC Dynamics Inc.
================================================
    F1  Help                  MAVIS BEACON TEACHES TYPING
    F2  Maintenance           MATH BLASTER PLUS
    F3                        WORD ATTACK PLUS
```

Completed Menu after first part of the installation.

Adding Selections to the Menu

The next program to add to the menu is *Algeblaster.* From the standard **Menu** screen:

1. Press **F2** for **Maintenance**

2. Use arrows to select **Menu**

3. Select **Menu Selection Maintenance** Press < Enter >

4. Type in the name of the **Menu, ED** and press < Enter >

5. Select **Add** and press < Enter >

6. Select **Run Program** and press < Enter >

7. Select **Edit** and press <Enter>

8. For **Selection** type **ALGEBLASTER**, press <Enter>

9. For **Directory** type **C:\Algebra** press <Enter>

10. For **Execute** type **Algebra** and press <Enter>

11. For **Password** press <Enter>

12. On the bottom of the screen select **Accept** and press <Enter>

This completes the installation of *Algeblaster* to the **Menu**. The other programs are installed in the same way.

6. Install *Math Blaster Mystery*

 Repeat procedures 1,2 and 3.

4. For **Selection** type **MATH BLASTER MYSTERY,** press <Enter>
5. For **Directory** type **C:\MBM**
6. For **Execute** type **MBM** and press <Enter>
7. For **Password** press <Enter>
8. On the bottom of the screen select **Accept** and press <Enter>

7. Install *Where in the World is Carmen Sandiego?*

Repeat procedures 1,2 and 3.

4. For **Selection** type **WHERE IN THE WORLD IS CARMEN SANDIEGO?,** press <Enter>
5. For **Directory** type **C:\World**
6. For **Execute** type **Carmen** and press <Enter>
7. For **Password** press <Enter>
8. On the bottom of the screen select **Accept** and press <Enter>

8. Install *Once Upon a Time*

Repeat procedures 1,2 and 3.

4. For **Selection** type **ONCE UPON A TIME,** press <Enter>
5. For **Directory** type **C:\ONCE**
6. For **Execute** type **ONCE** and press <Enter>
7. For **Password** press <Enter>
8. On the bottom of the screen select **Accept** and press <Enter>

9. Install *Microsoft Works*

Repeat procedures 1,2 and 3.

4. For **Selection** type **MICROSOFT WORKS,** press <Enter>
5. For **Directory** type **C:\WORKS**
6. For **Execute** type **WORKS** and press <Enter>
7. For **Password** press <Enter>
8. On the bottom of the screen select **Accept** and press <Enter>

CONGRATULATIONS!

 All of your programs are loaded. The menu is set up and ready to go. The next step will be to test each of the menu items to see that they actually start the programs. If any one of the programs doesn't run, repeat the **menu installation** process for that program. If that does not solve the problem, reinstall the program. (If you have to reinstall, first erase the current program, remove the directory and start over.)

---

[1]You will notice that different programs require different commands to install them on your hard disk. When you purchase any program, read the instruction manual for the installation procedure.

Chapter 9

Mathematics

For the Parent

MATHEMATICS

From buying groceries to launching spaceships, mathematics is the foundation of our scientific, economic and everyday life. A student who does not become knowledgeable in basic math enters society as an innumeric person -- one who cannot understand many of the principal functions or daily transactions that are part of our fabric of living. In our society there is a perverse pride in mathematical ignorance. Mathematical illiteracy is often flaunted: "I can't even balance my checkbook." "I'm a people person, not a number person." This lack of interest in math is reflected in our educational system. There is an acute shortage of math teachers. The subject is not given the same level of importance as word literacy. As a result, Americans are ranked tenth internationally on a measure of mathematical proficiency.

John Paulos, in his book *Innumeracy* recounts the story of a summer visitor in Maine who enters a hardware store and buys a large number of expensive items. The skeptical, reticent owner doesn't say a word as he adds the visitors bill on the cash register. When he's finished, he points to the total and watches as the man counts out $1,528.47 He then methodically recounts the money once, twice, three times. The visitor finally asks if he's given him the right amount of money, to which the Mainer grudgingly responds, "Just barely."

Using the **Computer Curriculum**, your child will build a basic mathematical foundation, an understanding of what numbers mean and a foundation for mathematical literacy.

Math Blaster Plus

The math programs for the **Computer Curriculum** were chosen because they are interesting, varied and use the basic principles that have been defined as the criteria for good educational software.   One criteria especially important in mathematics, is that the programs have many different levels of difficulty. Since the capabilities of students in the same grade or age group can vary significantly, the software must be able to allow for that factor.

Math Blaster Plus covers a range of exercises from addition to percentages. This program, with its outstanding graphics, is fun and interesting and thus self-motivating. It builds critical thinking skills and develops new concepts for the students.   The software takes multiple approaches to similar problems, with 30 different levels of difficulty so students can work at their own level. At the end of each lesson, the program prints out the students' scores. A **CERTIFICATE OF ACCOMPLISHMENT** can be printed when the student graduates from one level to the next. The program also maintains a complete record of students' scores and includes an editor which permits students to input their own math problems to help them prepare for a test.

Math Blaster Plus combines a problem-solving format with an action-packed arcade style game. With this software, the computer becomes a powerful tool for building a strong foundation in math. It allows children to work at their own pace enjoying success as they learn the basic building blocks of mathematics.

An animated Blasternaut ties the games together as he happily romps through outer space. Whether journeying through the cosmos or working at the recycling center, the Blasternaut captivates children making it fun to practice math. His friend, Spot, joins him as a sidekick through his adventures. In the final game, the Blasternaut and Spot must overcome the villainous trash aliens. This software helps to develop students self-confidence and sense of achievement, motivating them to keep working with the program.

This program consists of five different activities.

1. Rocket Launcher

Most students find practicing basic math a bore. Yet, as Howard Gardner says in **The Unschooled Mind,** "It is difficult to imagine how a young child could cope with the environment without incipient numerical capacities." In **Rocket Launcher** a concrete goal is established for knowing basic tables and equations. The object of the game is to build a rocket and launch it. If students answer the problem correctly, parts of the rocket appear on the launching pad. After all of the problems have been answered, the rocket is assembled. The Blasternaut gets into the rocket and blasts off. The program covers all levels of math, presenting equations in adding, subtraction, multiplication, division, fractions, decimals and percentages.

2. Trash Zapper

Math students using traditional study methods often find themselves learning formulas by rote, neither understanding the basic principals underlying the equations nor finding math in itself exciting. Students using **Trash Zapper** not only develop a greater understanding of the *meaning* of equations but, in a fun way, better prepare themselves both educationally and emotionally for higher level math courses, such as Algebra.

By finding missing values in equations, students earn points (zaps), which allow them (through the mighty Blasternaut) to clean up the space environment. (How many traditional study methods introduce the concept of environmental awareness into mathematics?)

3. Number Recycler

Even though four-year-olds appreciate the order (sequence) of number words and have a feel for basic relationships, like greater than or less than, this relational concept is often not developed in the same degree as language skills. Every day newspapers present us with numbers that need to be related to other numbers, but too many people do not understand what numerical relationships are. If one political candidate has 33% of the vote and the other has 39% , who is ahead? If one store is offering 20% off and another is having a third-off sale which one is better? Number Recycler helps the student learn some of the relationships that exist between numbers. It also teaches them about "recycling".

4. Math Blaster

In our contemporary society where everything moves at a fast pace, the ability to recognize numbers and their relationships in an instantaneous manner becomes very important. In the arcade style game *Math Blaster,* as problems appear on the screen students have only moments to make up their minds and find the correct answers. They must then transport the "Blasternaut" to the station in order to garner points.

For Parents and Students

Getting Started with *Math Blaster Plus*

At this point, you are ready to start setting up the program. As you prepare to use this software, ask your child to sit down at the computer while you explain the instructions for starting the program. After you have gone through the startup procedure together, your child should be able to repeat the process without your assistance. You may also find it helpful to read through the user's manual that comes with *Math Blaster Plus* and keep it handy for reference.

To start the program

MENU WORKS 2.1O

F1 HELP   **EDUCATION**
                        = = = = = = = = = = =
                        MATH BLASTER PLUS
                        WORD ATTACK PLUS
                        P C GLOBE
                        CARMEN SANDIEGO
                        OREGON TRAIL

---

    1. Move the lightbar on **MENU WORKS** to *Math Blaster Plus* and press < Enter >.

A new screen appears (see below) and asks you to enter your name. It is important that students type their names the same way each time so that record keeping will be consistent. To show this, we will use a student named Peter.

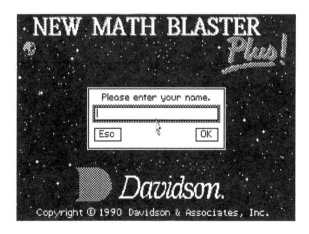

Type your name: (up to 20 letters) and press < Enter >
or click OK with the mouse.
Example:
   Peter < Enter >

The program asks for the date. If your computer has a built in clock with a calendar you need only press < Enter > or click OK and the date will be entered automatically. If not, press the arrow keys until the correct date appears. You can move between the boxes on the screen by using the **tab key**. When the correct date is in the box, press < Enter > or click OK.

After a cartoon, the ***Davidson Student Desktop Interface*** appears on the screen. (See below) It is a menu that provides flexibility in working with this software program.

DESKTOP INTERFACE
You can work with the desktop interface either using a mouse or the keyboard and function keys.

GETTING STARTED WITH THE PROGRAM

The desktop interface uses ``pull-down'' menus that work like window shades. On the top row of the interface is a menu bar. You can pull down the menu using the Function key (F2, F3 etc.) listed next to the activity you want. Once you have pulled down the menu, you can access any items listed on it using the mouse, or your up and down arrow keys, to move the light bar to the section you want. Pressing < Esc > will snap the shade back up.

The first thing you want to do is set-up record keeping:

Press F2 for (FILE). Move the lightbar down to record keeping. Press
<Enter>. This will select record keeping. A check mark will be on the
left side.

CHOSE THE RECORD will appear on the screen.

Chose the record with the student's name by clicking it with the mouse. If
the student is not listed, use the backspace key to clear the field and type in
the name (eight letters or less) and add **.rec** as an extension to indicate
record. (e.g. Peter.Rec) Press <Enter>. You are back to the student
menu.

The average ten to twelve year old will probably start this program in the
``Fractions, Decimals, and Percentages'' section. A student's level depends on his
or her ability to maintain scores of 85% or above on problems at that level. Neither
students nor parents should feel discouraged if this is below the student's present
grade level. The important thing is to build an excellent foundation in these types of
math problems because they are the problems we all run into in everyday life.
Understanding these problems will help with taxes, mortgages, and even with the
division of cherry pie.

Use the starting point test (located in Appendix B) to determine the level where
your student should begin.

1. Press **F4** and move the lightbar to the correct place (e.g. **Division**) and
    press <Enter>.

2. Next, press **F5** and based upon the starting point test, move the lightbar
    down to the appropriate level (e.g. **Level 3**) and press <Enter>.

Only two more steps and your student is ready to start the program.

First check the student's file for record keeping.

    3.   Press F2 to check that record keeping is on. (The check mark should be on the left.) Press <Esc> to close the shade.

The last step in setting the system up is turning on ``**Save Menu Defaults.**'' This means that when you start the program the next time, the computer will remember the activity and level at which the student was last working. To do this:

    4.   Pull down the file menu with your mouse or use the **F2** key. Then, move the lightbar down until **Save Menu Defaults** is highlighted. Click the mouse or press <Enter>.
The **Save Menu Defaults** box will appear.

    5.   If the items are correct, using your mouse, click on **Save Defaults** or, if you are using a keyboard, tab over to it and press <Enter>.

You are now ready to start the program.

Be sure to let the student do the preceding start-up steps as you explain them. This will allow students to work with *MATH BLASTER PLUS* independently.

USING THE ACTIVITIES

Rocket Launcher

This activity reinforces math facts as it uses exciting drills to teach basic math skills.

There are two levels to *Rocket Launcher*.

The first option is the Study level. It shows the full equation so students see the answer before solving the problem.

The second is the Solve level. It gives only the equation challenging the student to solve it by finding the answer.

Study Option

Use the up arrow to highlight, or the mouse to click, the **Study option.** A problem and its solution will appear on the screen.

example:
$$10 + 8 = 18$$

Press the spacebar on the keyboard to make the answer disappear.

$$10 + 8 = \underline{\qquad}$$

Type the correct answer into the equation and press <Enter>.

To get out of the program at any time press <ESC>.

Solve Option

Using the arrow keys or the mouse, the student should now go back to the *Math Blaster Menu* (main screen) and do the same exercise in the Solve mode without seeing the answers before working the problem.

Click ***Rocket Launcher***
Click ***Solve it***

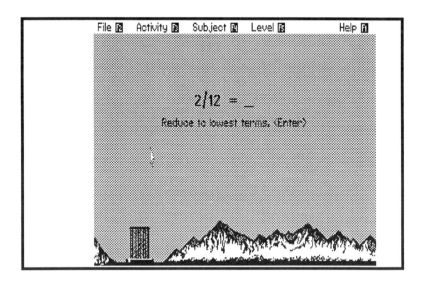

example:

    2/12   = _____

    Type the correct answer into the equation and press < Enter >.
If the answer is incorrect, a **Try Again** message will appear. After two incorrect tries, the correct answer will appear on the screen.

    If the student answers correctly, parts of a rocket will appear on the launch pad and begin to be assembled. After all the problems have been answered correctly, the rocket is assembled. The Blasternaut gets into the rocket and blasts off.

    As the program will repeat all the missed problems, the rocket cannot take off until the student has solved 100% of the problems.

A scoreboard is displayed at the end of the activity. Students who get 100% can print a certificate of completion. Students receiving less than 100% can print a scorecard. (Remember to turn record keeping on at the beginning of the program so the score will be saved.)

Students scoring less than 85% on the program should move to the **Retake** section. Those scoring more than 85%, can move on to the next level. Or, to view the problems in another manner, they can go back to the menu screen and select *Trash Zapper.*

Trash Zapper

The goal of the *Trash Zapper* is to find a missing value in an equation. If the student gets the correct answer the Blasternaut will clean up the space environment.

example: **3/4 + ?   =   1**

Type the missing number (**1/4**) and press <Enter>.

If the student answers incorrectly twice, the correct answer will appear on the screen.

Two zaps (shots) are awarded for each correct answer.
          Use the arrows to aim the laser scope at the trash
          Press the spacebar to zap the cosmic garbage.

The scoreboard for this activity is the same as the one for *Rocket Launcher.* Students scoring less than 85% should repeat the exercise. Those scoring more than 85%, may go to the main screen and start the *Number Recycler.*

Number Recycler

On the *Math Blaster* Menu, use the <Tab> key or the mouse to move to *Number Recycler*. Press <Enter> or click with the mouse to start the program.

The *Number Recycler* is designed to build pattern recognition and the ability to plan ahead for the use of resources. In this game, students take risks, analyze number combinations, and make decisions.

The **Subject** menu and **Level** menu are not used in *Number Recycler*.

At the start of this activity a **Choose the subject** box appears. Use the arrow keys or mouse to select the subject. Press <Enter> or click OK.

The object of the game is to get to the next round by creating the required number of equations. Students help the Blasternaut make equations contained within the recycling machine.

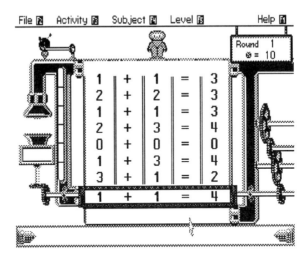

First, students analyze the numbers and find the equation that can be obtained with the least number of moves. This requires mentally moving first one column and then another to see what provides the best pattern.

```
4 * 4  =    9
0 * 3  =   12
4 * 4  =    8
0 * 2  =    4

1  * 2  =   0
```

Using the arrow keys, move the Blasternaut until he is above the column where a number or symbol is to be moved. (In the example above, we would want him in the leftmost column to push the **0** down one level.)

_   Press the down arrow keys to push the numbers or symbols down in a column.

_   Press < Enter > when a correct equation appears in the window.

```
0  *  2  =  0

press  < Enter >
```

If a number or symbol is pushed into the recycling chamber, it may be reused. If it is pushed down two spaces into the zap chamber, it's gone forever.
If after pushing a number or symbol down, students realize they have made a mistake then:

Press < CTRL > U to undo the last move.

To end the round, just press < CTRL > C.

As students play ***Number Recycler***, coins are earned for each correct equation. If they complete ten rounds, they can print a certificate of achievement.

The subject or round can be changed. If the equations are too easy, students can activate the Options from the Activity menu by pressing <CTRL>O. When they complete this exercise, they can return to the main menu by pressing <ESC> and tabbing to *MATH BLASTER.*

MATH BLASTER

In this arcade-style math game a problem appears on the screen with answers inside four different space stations. With limited time, while avoiding flying objects, students must navigate the Blasternaut to the space station with the correct answer. The Blasternaut can fly all over the screen using the arrow keys.

If five of the space-stations are entered correctly, a bonus round begins. The Blasternaut must fly through food items appearing on the screen to collect bonus points. The bonus round lasts until the alien reaches Spot. Then, regular play resumes. There are five phases with ten problems. Upon completion press <ESC> to return to the main menu.

The length of time a student spends on *MATH BLASTER PLUS* can vary but I suggest a minimum of one-half hour per session. Students who enjoy the program may continue for up to an hour. However, they should not be allowed to become distracted from the other learning programs included in this curriculum.

Viewing a Student's Record

At the end of each exercise/game, the program records the student's score. You can look at the student's scores by pressing <F2>. When the correct directory is displayed, move the light bar to highlight the name of the file to be viewed (the students name will be in the file) and press <Enter>. The first page of the student's record will appear on the screen. To view other records use the arrow keys.

You can print the record at the point where the directory of the correct drive is displayed. Use the arrow keys or mouse to scroll down to highlight the name of the file to be printed and press <Enter>. To print the whole file, <Tab> or move the mouse to the print button and press <Enter>. (The default is to print all records). Press <Enter> again or click OK.

The record printed will look like this.

Record file:	Peter.Rec
Date	July 2, 1992
Activity	Rocket Launcher
Subject	Addition
Level	1
Score	92%

****

Esc   Print

Keep the printed copy in a file or notebook.

Using the Editor

In many instances, students encounter difficulty with certain types of math functions. There are also problems that a student may need to practice for a test. For these types of problems, Math Blaster Plus has an editor which lets you customize the program for an individual student's needs. (See the *Math Blaster* manual for detailed instructions.)

Summary

In this section, we have covered the major functions of *MATH BLASTER PLUS*. Using this program, students will develop basic skills in math that will serve them in life as well as future studies. When students complete all sections of this program with a score of 85% or better, they are ready to graduate to the next mathematical program.

ALGE-BLASTER PLUS

For the Parent

The next program your student will use is *ALGE-BLASTER PLUS*. This program has fewer games but does present algebra in a way that is easy for students to understand. *ALGE-BLASTER PLUS* provides a step-by-step approach to algebra, motivating students with learning tips and helpful hints as they work the problems. Besides the standard algebra problems, it also creates an approach for developing algebraic formulas for word problems. This is an excellent program to parallel any pre-algebra or algebra course offered in middle school or high school.

There are five major parts to the algebra program.

> **Learn:** This is where the student learns the basic steps in solving an equation.

> **Solve:** Once students know the steps in working with equations, this section will give them practice solving the equations covered in **Learn**.

> **Translate:** Converting word expressions, or life problems, into algebraic expressions.

> **Graph:** Practicing working with points and slopes.

> **Alge-Blaster Plus Game:** Students protect the space station by applying basic graphing skills developed in the graph activity. Unfortunately, this game is the least helpful part of **ALGE-BLASTER PLUS** but students can play it for their own amusement.

For the Student and Parent

What You Will Learn

The **Learn** and **Solve** sections of **ALGE-BLASTER PLUS** will introduce the basics of algebra. This will help build a foundation for the more advanced portions of the program as well as future studies in mathematics. The basics that ALGE-BLASTER PLUS will introduce are:

Integers: Adding, subtracting, multiplying and dividing.

Example: $+4 - (-3)$

Order of operations: Using rules to solve equations.

Example: $+4 -2 * 8 / 4$

Monomials and Polynomials: Combining and simplifying using the four basic operations, add, subtract, multiply and divide.

Example: $4x - 6y + y - x + 3xy$

Factoring: Recognizing and applying fundamental forms.

Example: $8x + 2x$

Equations: Evaluating expressions and linear equations containing positive integral exponents, as well as linear equations containing integers, fractions and decimals.

Example: $x - 3 = 14$

Systems of Equations: Solving systems of linear equations.

Examples: $7x + 3y = 19$
$4x - 3y = 3$

Other Functions

Algebraic Fractions: Combining and simplifying using the basic operations.

Radicals: Simplifying and using the basic operations.

Quadratic Equations: Solving problems by factoring and using the quadratic formula.

Starting the Program

For the Student

To start the program move the lightbar on the menu to *Alge-Blaster Plus* and press < Enter >. The screen then asks for your name. It is important that you enter your name the same way each time so that the record keeping will be consistent.

Enter your name: (up to 20 letters) and press < Enter > or click OK with the mouse.

The Davidson Student Desktop Interface then comes to the screen. This interface works in the same manner as the one in *Math Blaster Plus*.

Beginning to Work with the Program

As you begin the program you will see a menu bar at the top row of the interface. You can move around the menu bar by using the horizontal arrow keys or by pulling down the menu with your mouse. Once you have pulled down the menu, or activated it by pressing the correct function key, you can access any items on the menu by using the mouse or your vertical arrow keys to move the light bar up or down.

1.   Pull down the **File menu** or press <F2>.

2.   Move the lightbar to **Record Keeping**.

3.   Press <Enter>.

This will activate a dialogue box in which you have the choice of creating a new record if its the first time you've worked with the program or adding to an existing record if you have done these exercises before.

1.   Use the mouse to select.

2.   Press <Enter> for OK.

If it is the first time you've used the program, type your name for the file name.

In our example, the name of the file will be:

\algebra\peter

Click ``**check file**'' to turn record keeping on.

Press <ESC> to release the pull down menu then, based upon the preliminary test, set the subject and level.

Example: 1. Pull down **Subject menu.**

2. Move light bar to **Factoring.**

3. Press <Enter>.

4. Choose level 1, which is already set.

The Activity will now start on Factoring, Level 1.

Activity 1 Learn

The objective of the **Learn** activity is to present a step-by-step procedure for solving algebra problems. This tutorial shows the basic steps students must take to solve an algebraic problem, provides practice in doing such problems, defines important algebraic concepts and terms and shows examples of them.

1.   Highlight the **Learn** icon on the menu screen.

2.   Select a subject from the menu bar e.g. **Equations.**

3.   Select a Level from the **Level** menu.

4.   Press <Enter> or click the **Learn** icon

First, an example problem is shown with an explanation of each step and the final solution. The program will let you work at your own pace allowing you to move back to the previous step (or problem) to review. After the example, there are three similar problems that you can work. If you have trouble, go back to the example.

Illustration of Screen
Example: Adding Integers.

-4 + (-8)

When numbers have the same
sign, add the numbers and use the sign.

Previous   Next

Study the problem and the text that appears below it.

1. Click **Next** when you are ready to continue.

Study the first step and the explanation of how this step was reached.

2. Select **Next** to continue.

Continue to study each step of the problem. The number of steps for each example problem may be different.

3. To review any steps click **Previous**.

After the example problem, there are three practice problems along with instructions for the first step needed to solve each problem.

4. Read the problem and the instructions for the first step and select **Next.**

5. Enter the solution to the first step. Press <Enter>.

If you input the wrong answer twice, the correct answer will appear on the screen.

6. Press <Enter> for the next step.

7. Study the next step and press <Enter> or click OK.

8. Enter the second step solution, then press <Enter>.

Continue with the steps until you have solved the problem.

In entering the steps, you will find that the cursor automatically moves from one input area of the equation to another. This appears a little unusual at first, but you'll find that you get used to it very quickly.

Special Algebraic Characters

Some answers may require use of special algebraic characters (symbols) which are displayed at the bottom of the screen. They can be activated in the following manner:

- To use a special character, put the cursor at the desired location of the character.

- Press <Ctrl> and the appropriate numbered function key (F1-F5) at the same time.

Plus/Minus Sign:

<Ctrl> F1 The plus/minus sign will be displayed on the screen. (This may look different from other equations)

Example: The square root of 4 is +/- 2

Square Root Radical:

<Ctrl> F2 The square root radical expands as you enter numbers.

To turn this function off press <Ctrl> F2 again. (This is a toggle switch)

Exponent:

<Ctrl> F3 Enter an exponent.

To exit the exponent mode, press the right arrow key.

Numerator:

<Ctrl> F4 Enter the numerator. Press the right arrow key to move the cursor to the denominator: enter the denominator.

To exit the fraction mode, press the right arrow key again.

Small Fractions:

<Ctrl> F5 The small fraction key allows you to include small fractions within larger fractions.

Enter the numerator first. Press the right arrow to move the cursor to the denominator: enter the denominator.

Press the right arrow key to exit the fraction mode.

If you want to review any of the steps, press <Ctrl> R and select previous to continue moving backwards. After the practice problems you can press any key to return to the main screen.

To quit an activity, press <Esc> or select Stop from the Activity menu.

Activity 2   Solve

The object of the **Solve** activity is to give you a chance to practice the concepts and skills that are acquired in the **Learn** activity. You will practice applying these skills by solving each problem on your own. Problems should be solved on paper first with only the final answer entered into the computer. This activity reinforces the concepts and sorts of problems illustrated in **Learn**.

Highlight the **Solve** icon on the **Main screen.**

Select a subject from the **Subject** menu

Select a level from the **Level** menu

Select **Start** from the **Activity** menu if you want to begin with a particular problem. (Maintain a notebook in order to remember which problem you did last.)

Press < Enter > or click the **Solve** icon.

You can now select either **Practice With Help** or **Solve On Your Own.** (Start with Solve On Your Own; if that turns out to be too difficult, go to Practice With Help)

Solve on Your Own

Study the problem on the screen

Solve the problem using pencil and paper if necessary.

Type in the answer and press < Enter >.

You have two chances before the correct answer is supplied.

Press < Enter > to go to the next problem.

There are ten to fifteen problems in each set. When you complete the problems, the scorecard appears. Press any key to return to the Main screen.

Practice with Help

In this mode you can ask for a hint.

> Type the answer and press <Enter>.

> If you want help, select **Hints** from the Student Aid menu or press <Ctrl> H.

> If you'd like more help, click **Next** to see the next hint.

> To leave the hint box select OK.

> Enter the final answer and press <Enter>.

> Press <Enter> to go to the next problem.

Activity 3 Translate

The **Translate** activity prepares you for solving algebraic word problems. This is a multiple choice activity in which you will learn to set up an equation by translating words into algebraic equations and ultimately equations into words. You will get a better understanding of math symbols and vocabulary used in word problems. As a result you will also learn the value of variables.

Example: The quotient of a number x and 98 is a number y diminished by 16.

The skills involved in this program are more complex and closer to real life problems than those in the previous sections. You must carefully read and study the problem and then interpret it to set up an algebraic expression and/or equation. To accomplish this, you must understand the phrases *more than, decreased by, product of, quotient of,* etc.

NOTE: there is a section in the Menu Bar where you can find definitions of the math terms used in this program.

Move the lightbar to **Student Aid F6** and press < Enter >
Move the lightbar to **Terms** and press < Enter >

Example: The absolute value is the value of the number without the sign, (e.g. the numbers 9 and -9 both have an absolute value of 9.)

To Start Translate:

Highlight the **Translate** icon on the Menu.
(The subject menu is not used with this activity.)

Select level: Only three levels are available in this exercise.

Press < Enter > or click the **Translate** icon.

Select a format option:

Choose equation
Choose phrase
Mixed

Example: **Choose phrase**

Choose Phrase
Read the phrase or equation at the top of the screen:

> Enter the letter before the correct answer, or click the correct answer with the mouse, or, using the arrow keys, move the lightbar to the correct answer
>
> Press <Enter>.

Activity 4 Graph

The objective of the **Graph** activity is to familiarize you with the coordinate system and slopes of lines. As you develop these graphing skills, you can better visualize the mathematical relationships illustrated on a graph.

Learning Math Terminology

To use the **Graph** activity you will be required to know the definitions of key math terms including: *graph, coordinate system, slope, quadrant, point, axis, line, and ordered pair.* You should look up these terms in an Algebra textbook or within the program by pressing the **<F6>** key and moving the lightbar to the term you want.

Beginning to Work with Graphs

In level 1 you will learn about coordinate systems by locating and labeling points on a graph. You will begin to draw conclusions about these points and understand the meaning of axis, quadrants and negative numbers.

You will learn to visualize ordered pairs, locate positions on a graph, calculate slopes and (given the slope and another point) find a point.   (In this activity the subject menu is not available.)

Find a Point

An ordered pair e.g. (5, -1) is given. The first number represents the x axis and the second number the y axis. In this example you would use your arrows to move 5 spaces to the right (positive) on the x axis and then 1 down (negative) on the y axis.

Label a Point

In this activity, count the number of spaces to the right (positive) or left (negative) on the x axis and the number of up (positive) or down (negative) spaces on the y axis and enter the numbers.

Level 2

In Level 2, you will learn to find the slope of a line or find a second point if a point and a slope are given.

Click **Find Slope**

Calculate the slope by using the formula

Example: slope = y2 - y1 / x 2 - x 1

If the first point is (3, 2) and the second (5, 4), then the slope would be (4-2)/(5-3) = 2/2 or 1. Enter the slope with a slash between the two numbers.

Printing a Record

At the end of each session press <F2> or click **File** and move the lightbar to **Print record.** Press <Enter> and click name.

Note: When I first tried to print a record, a message came up asking for a file that the program could not find. The problem was that the program was not set up for the right printer. If you encounter that problem:

               Press <F10>
               Click setup.
               Press <F2> for the Options menu and move the lightbar down to printer.
               Press <Enter> and select ASCII as the printer. That is the only

printer that will work with this program.

Summary: In the two sections of this chapter we have covered basic math (Level 1 and 2) and the more complex aspects of math covered in an Algebra class. The student that fully understands these two programs will have an excellent founding in mathematics and the use of numbers for many types of problems.

Chapter 10

Building Vocabulary
with *WORD ATTACK PLUS*

For the Parent

As Mark Twain once remarked, the difference between using the right word and the wrong word can be the difference between lightning and a lightning bug.

In everything from speaking to writing we are often judged by the vocabulary we use. The better we can understand what we read and the more creatively we use a variety of words that adeptly convey our ideas, the more successful we will be. Vocabulary is the cornerstone to a successful education. Ideas are only as good as we are at expressing them. Building vocabulary means not only building the number of words we can use, but the quality of the ideas we can create and discuss. A rich vocabulary is an invaluable possession in life. It will give students an edge in school today and in their chosen profession in the future. Repeated studies have shown that the vocabulary of top management and leaders is greater than that of their subordinates. Vocabulary is intimately tied up with success. With this program, students will build their vocabularies to help them achieve their goals in school and in their careers.

American students in general and, regrettably, the cream of the academic crop in particular are not as verbally proficient as past generations of college applicants. In the years between 1970 and 1980, the scores on the verbal Scholastic Aptitude Test (SAT) declined, especially at the top level. The SAT exam for ``advanced vocabulary knowledge'' is an important part of the entrance criteria for most major colleges. One of the goals of the Computer Curriculum is to help students prepare for college. This chapter is crucial to achieving that goal.

Without the vocabulary to express their thoughts, students ideas remain trapped in their minds. Because they cannot communicate their thoughts students may become frustrated, causing their grades to suffer. As E.D. Hirsch Jr. says in his book, *Cultural Literacy*: ``A universally shared vocabulary is analogous to a universal currency like the dollar.'' Unless students have the proper vocabulary they can neither understand nor express the ideas of the 21st century.

In this section and the word processing chapter associated with it, the **Computer Curriculum** will help develop a vocabulary that will permit students to share their ideas with their teachers, their fellow students and the world.

There are many ways to build a vocabulary. Reading, listening and memorizing word lists are some of the traditional methods. The most important factor is to develop an awareness of words. There are two types of vocabulary; a receptive vocabulary, which contains words you recognize when you read or listen; and an expressive vocabulary, which contains words you use in speaking or writing. In this chapter, we will be working with the receptive vocabulary. However, it is important for students to continue to develop their vocabulary by using the words they learn here as part of their expressive vocabulary when they write and speak.

Word Attack Plus

Word Attack Plus is a vocabulary building program that meets the criteria for good educational software. A true *tutorial program* with outstanding graphics, it is fun, interesting and therefore self-motivating. It is a five-part vocabulary building program that introduces over 700 words. In *Word Display,* a word is shown with its definition and usage in a sentence, laying the first block in building a base vocabulary.   The *Multiple Choice* portion of the program has a two-pronged approach, giving a definition with a choice of possible words or a word with a choice of possible definitions. The *Word Match* section matches a word with its definition as well as allowing the student to review other words in the group. Finally in *Sentence Completion*, the student is challenged to use the right word to complete a sentence.

The software incorporates multiple approaches to learning new vocabulary with ten different levels of difficulty. The program maintains a complete record of the students' scores. At the end of any lesson the score can be printed along with a *Certificate of Accomplishment* when a level is completed. This gives students positive reinforcement as they progress. An editor permits students to input their own vocabulary words to help them prepare for a quiz at school, or to record new words they have obtained by reading a book. Finally an action-packed, arcade-style game allows the computer to become a powerful tool for building a strong foundation for reading and writing.

Word Attack Plus lets students work at their own pace, enjoying success as they learn the basic building blocks of language.

Getting Started with *Word Attack Plus*

For the Parent and Student

At this point, you are ready to start setting up the program. It is useful to proceed with the following steps. As you prepare to use this software, ask your child to sit down at the computer while you explain the instructions for starting the program. You will find that after you have talked through the startup procedure, your child will be able to do it without your assistance. While following the instructions, you may also find it helpful to read through the user's manual that comes with *Word Attack Plus* and keep it handy for reference.

(Students appearing comfortable with this type of program can proceed on their own. After this point we will be talking to the student.)

For the Student

Starting from the menu, move the lightbar to **WORD ATTACK PLUS** and press <Enter>. The screen then asks for your name. It is important that you type your name the same way each time so that the name will be consistent in the record keeping section. As an example, we will use a student named Peter.

Enter your name: (up to 20 letters) and press <Enter>
or click OK with the mouse.

C: > **Peter** <Enter> or click OK

The program asks for the date, which is also important for accurate record keeping. If your computer has a built in clock with a calendar, you need only press <Enter> or click OK three times and the date will be set automatically. If your computer does not have a built in clock, press the arrow key until the correct date appears. You can move between the boxes in this form by using the <Tab> key. When you have the correct date, just press <Enter> or click OK.

Working with DESKTOP

The **DAVIDSON STUDENT DESKTOP INTERFACE**, which we refer to simply as **DESKTOP**, then comes on the screen. It is another type of menu that provides tremendous flexibility in working with this software.

You can work with the **DESKTOP** and the educational program, either using a mouse or the keyboard. A mouse works best with this program. Descriptions of how to work with **DESKTOP** and **WORD ATTACK PLUS** will be given with use of the mouse in mind.

On the top row of the **DESKTOP** there is a menu bar. The **DESKTOP** uses "pull-down" menus. A pull-down menu works like a window shade. When you move the cursor to the menu and click the mouse button, the menu comes down and a list of choices appear. Release the mouse button and the shade snaps back up so that it will be out of the way. Or, move the arrow to the field that you want to pull down and holding the mouse button down move the lightbar to the level or instruction you want activated. If you release the button at that point, the level or item will be activated.

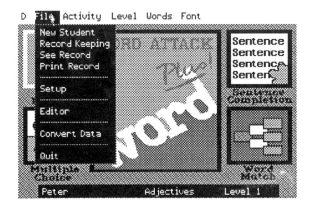

145

You can activate the menu bar without using the mouse by pressing <Esc>. Move around the menu by using your left and right arrows. When you reach the activity you want use the up and down arrows to highlight the level or item. Pressing <Enter> will activate that item.

Now that you are at the **DESKTOP**, the first thing to do is ``Setup.''

Move the cursor to **File**. Press the button and, holding it down, pull the lightbar to Setup and release the button. The Setup screen will appear.

You can move around in this screen only by use of the <Tab> key. Notice the little dash in the box. That is the cursor. As you press the <Tab> key the cursor moves to the next box.

Most systems today have a parallel printer. So, leave the P for parallel and tab to the next box.

If you have an IBM PC or a 286 PC clone you can probably leave the speed alone. If you have a 386 machine, you may want to enter 5000 in the Speed section. This will slow down the game. If you find it too slow, you can always increase the speed by returning to this part of Setup.

To update the record file you created a file called RECORD in the directory Therefore the path is C: > WAP\RECORD.

Use the backspace key to clear anything that may be in this space and type C: > \WAP\RECORDS

The new data file was called NEWDATA in the directory. Therefore the path is C: > WAP\NEWDATA.

Type C: > WAP\NEWDATA in as you did with RECORDS. When you have completed these updates, press <Enter> to save what you have just typed on the screen.

You now have two more items to set before you start the program.

Move the cursor to **File** on the menu bar and press the mouse button. The window will come down. Hold the button and move the lightbar to **Record keeping.** Release the mouse button and **Record keeping** will be activated.

Next, use the mouse to move to **Level** on the menu bar. Press the mouse key and hold it down. Based upon the score you had on the pre-test, move the lightbar down to your current level and release the mouse button.

The pre-test will give you a good idea for a starting point. Neither you nor your parent should feel discouraged if the level as determined by the pre-test is below your present grade level. The important thing is to **build** an excellent vocabulary. Your vocabulary is your projection lens to the world. It must be finely ground and well focused to have its greatest impact.

We have just gone over the procedure of how to set up the program. If you are having trouble with it ask your parents for assistance.

Using the Activities

1. Word Display

The purpose of this activity is to present a word with its definition and then show how the word is used in a sentence. There is a delay between the initial presentation of the word and its definition to give students a chance to think of the definition on their own.

Begin *Word Display* at the *Desktop* menu.

Move the mouse arrow to the *Word Display* box and click.

Each word, a brief definition and a sentence showing the correct usage is displayed on the screen. Read the word, the definition and the sentence. If it does not seem clear read it again and study it. Then press < space bar > for the next word.

When you have reached the end of this program, it returns to the ***Desktop***.
If the words appeared too easy, you can move up one level in difficulty.

Move the mouse to **Level** on the Menu bar and pull down the menu. Pull the lightbar
to the next level and release the button. Repeat the ***Word Display*** program.

2. Multiple Choice

An excellent way to reinforce what you have learned is to try to
recall it. This helps place it in long term memory as well as allowing
you to develop the right retrieval method for recalling the word.
Multiple Choice is a fun way to practice these techniques..

If the level appears correct at the ***Desktop***, you're ready to begin.

Move the arrow to ***Multiple Choice*** and click the mouse.

The screen will give you 2 choices. Choose **Display the Word** to select the
correct meaning of the given word. To select the correct word for the given
definition, choose **Display the meaning**.

Move the mouse to choose **Definition** and click.

The definition screen will appear.

```
                    fragile

        A       very tired
        B       having to do with cities
        C       easily broken
        D       very strong
```

There are three ways to indicate the correct answer on this screen.

Move the mouse to the correct answer and click.

Type the correct letter (in this case the letter **C**).

Use the arrows to move the lightbar down to the correct answer and press <Enter>.

If your answer is correct, another question will appear. If not, the message "Try again" will appear on the screen. If your second answer is also wrong, the correct answer will be highlighted for you.

When you have finished the lesson, a scoreboard will appear. It will show the percentage of correct answers. Questions answered on the second try are worth only half as much as those answered correctly the first time.

Press <Space bar> to continue. The program will ask you if you want to retake the questions you missed. Answer Y (yes) and redo the ones you missed.

The key to determine if you are ready to move ahead to the next level is the first score. If you have completed the program and your score is below 85% you should go back to the main menu. If your score is above 85%, you can move on to the next level or to the main screen.

3. Sentence Completion

For the parent

This is the most difficult of the activities because it requires recalling a word from memory, determining its correct usage and spelling the word. This activity starts to cross the line between passive and active vocabulary making it a very important exercise. However, because of its difficulty, I recommend that this activity be put off until last to give students time to become more familiar with the words and their meanings. They should do the **Word Match** exercise and play the **Word Attack Plus** game prior to tackling this exercise.

For the student

Sentence Completion starts by putting the meaning of a word at the top of the screen. A sentence appears with a blank space where a word must be typed. Type the correct word into the blank space. It must be one of the words in your other exercises at this level. If you misspell the word, it will be considered incorrect.

If you can't recall the word or its spelling you can get help by pressing <Ctrl>H for a hint. A list of twelve words from the current lesson will appear at the bottom of the screen. You can choose the correct answer from the list but must type it with the correct spelling.

At the end of the program, a Scoreboard shows the percentage of correct answers. You probably won't achieve an 85% on the first pass. Missed answers should be redone and the entire activity repeated until a score of 85% is achieved. At that point, continue to the next step.

4. Word Match

In this activity, words are displayed on the screen in overlapping boxes. You can access only one layer of boxes at a time.

Move the mouse to the word you want to select and click it.

Move the mouse to the arrows on the bottom of the screen and click on them to scroll through until you find the correct definition. You can also use the arrow keys for this purpose.

When you find the correct definition press < Enter >

This removes the word from the screen and a new box (word) becomes accessible in the layer beneath. Continue until all the boxes have been removed from the screen.

Matching words to definitions is similar to *Multiple Choice*. At the start you have the possibility of 20 different answers but as you move along fewer remain. When you finish this exercise, you will have had another go around with the words from this level. These words and their meanings will begin to be more and more familiar to you.

5. WORD ATTACK PLUS Game.

This arcade-type game reinforces learning in an entertaining way. In starting the game you are given a choice of three speeds. Until you are more familiar with the game, set it at the Regular speed. Use the right and left arrows on the keyboard to move the ``Hattacker'' (on the white band) directly under the word that matches the definition at the bottom of the screen. Press < spacebar > to make him throw one of his hats at the proper word. A timer is displayed. To earn points you must match the definition before the time runs out. The points you receive vary according to the type of hat thrown. Additional points can be earned by helping the Hattacker catch other hats as they move across the screen. This is done by moving him under the hat and pressing the < spacebar >.

By forcing you to react quickly, this game keeps new words in your active memory. You will be surprised as the new words you have just learned come to mind when you are writing papers, book reports, and even in everyday conversation.

The length of time you spend on *Word Attack Plus* can vary but I suggest a minimum of thirty minutes per session. If you are enjoying it, continue for up to an hour but this should not distract you from the other programs that are included in your curriculum.

For the Parent

NOTE: When the student completes one level, print out a list of the 20 words in that section. (see Print Flash cards.) Use these words in *Once Upon a Time* or *Word Processing.*

Viewing a Student's Record

At the end of each exercise or game, the program records the student's score. You can then look at the scores using the mouse.

Pull down the File menu and use the arrows to highlight **View Record,** press <Enter> or click the mouse. When the correct directory is displayed, move the bar to highlight the name of the file to be viewed and press <Enter>. The first page of the student's record will appear on the screen. To view other pages, use the arrows or drag the scroll bar.

To print the record move the lightbar to the correct drive, press the arrows or scroll down and highlight the name of the file to be printed and press <Enter>. To print the whole file, <Tab> or move the mouse to the print button and press <Enter>. (The default is to print all records). Press <Enter> again or click OK with the mouse.

Take the printed copy, three hole punch it and put it into the notebook set up in the record keeping section.

Next Step

Once all five activities in **WORD ATTACK PLUS** have been completed, return to the main menu.

Move the mouse to **Words** on the menu bar, click the mouse, pull it down to the next group and release the button.

The first group of words are adjectives followed by nouns and then verbs. There are a total of 60 words on each level.

TIME: Each session on this program should consist of one level for each type of word. For example, level 4- adjectives would be one session. When starting the next session students should repeat any level where their score was below 85%.

For review, have students run at least one **Multiple Choice** exercise to make certain the words are retained. Students who don't remember the words should repeat the entire level.

REMEMBER: THE PURPOSE IS NOT HOW FAST YOU CAN ADVANCE BUT HOW WELL YOU CAN LEARN THE VOCABULARY.

Using the Editor

In many instances students have problems with certain words or types of words. There are also words and definitions that a student may need to practice for a test. For these situations, there is an editor function which allows you to set up individualized exercises in *WORD ATTACK PLUS*. See the manual for details.

Chapter Summary

For Students and Parents

I cannot over-emphasize the importance of verbal skills in a student's life. The level of vocabulary children are exposed to by the ubiquitous television is very limited. TV shows are designed to reach the lowest common denominator in the home audience -- generally someone with no more than an eighth grade education. Only by reading books and magazines and studying vocabulary, can a student prepare for college and a rewarding career.

Our world is changing rapidly and adults in virtually every walk of life have to learn new skills to keep up with transformations in technology and society. The best way to prepare for and cope with these changes is through reading. In order to profit from this reading one must possess a first rate vocabulary.

Chapter 11

Decision Making, Critical Thinking and Deductive Reasoning

For the Parent

What Is Decision Making Software?

Each day we make decisions about everything from what type of toothbrush we want to use, to who to vote for in the elections. Oftentimes we make these decisions because of a gut feeling we have, an intuition that one choice is better than the other. We make our choices not necessarily because of a logical and cogent argument that says one is better than the other, but because one choice feels right and the other does not. It seems to make more sense to buy a red toothbrush than a blue one.

There are other ways to make decisions. You might make a decision by doing research or asking questions. You might read *Consumer Reports* to find which toothbrush does the best job of removing plaque, or asks your dentist for his recommendation. In terms of voting you might look at the candidates voting record rather than judge by appearances or campaign promises.

By asking these kinds of questions and gathering information you make a decision based upon that information, not just gut instinct. You will have developed a decision support system which provides a framework for making the most logical choices.

What is the difference between the two approaches to making decisions? In one instance, you made a knee jerk decision. In the second, you developed a series of questions to gather facts and opinions that caused you to think through the factors determining your decision. This is fundamental decision making. In this chapter, you will learn how three software packages can help your child develop this important life skill.

Where does this ability to do research and make informed decisions come from? There is no class in high school on decision making. There may be a hint of the concept in science, but generally science is taught by telling students the conclusions scientists have reached, paying very little attention to the scientific methods used to reach these conclusions. Students learn little about the original thinking process, which was composed of many questions and facts that led to a hypothesis. A hypothesis is a question asked of the world. The scientist must help find the answer.

Critical thinking is the process of identifying key factors in any situation. It is the methodology of formulating a scientific hypothesis, of determining which political candidate to vote for or of deciding what career path you should follow. It will give the student the ability to identify misleading advertising and to weigh competing evidence.

The decision making games introduced here, *Where in the World is Carmen Sandiego?*, *Oregon Trail* and *Math Blaster Mystery,* can help develop the concept of gathering facts and information in order to make intelligent decisions. It doesn't matter if it's a question regarding which plane to take to chase *Carmen Sandiego,* how much money to spend to get a raft to float across the river on the *Oregon Trail,* or which information to use in order to solve the problems in *Math Blaster Mystery.* The concept of decision making is the same.

In *Math Blaster Mystery,* word problems deal with real situations that present the information needed to solve the problems as well as some extraneous facts that appear to be important but are not needed to get the correct answer. Students must decide what information they need to solve the problem and what is *noise* and has no relevance.

In *Carmen Sandiego,* students must gather information and make decisions as to when they have enough information to apply for a warrant to go after the criminal.

When traveling the *Oregon Trail,* students must watch food supplies, health and weather, decide when to rest or cut back on food rations and take care of their companions. The decisions they must make will mean life or death to their companions.

All of these programs cause students to gather information, and make decisions, forcing them **to think.**

To the Student

TRAVELING THE OREGON TRAIL

In this program, you will bid farewell to friends and neighbors and set off on a 2,000-mile trek in a covered wagon. Do you want to be a banker, farmer or carpenter? This decision will affect your trip and your ability to handle problems along the trail. As you travel, many more decisions will have to be made. This will be good training for the time when you have to make major decisions in your life, including your choice of a career.

The first screen looks like this:

The Oregon Trail
****

YOU MAY ..
1. **Travel the trail**
2. **Learn about the trail**
3. **See the Oregon Top Ten**
4. **Turn sound off**
5. **Choose Management options**
6. **End**

What is your choice ? ____

****

Select number **2** to **Learn about the Oregon trail**. Type the number **2** and press <Enter>. The screen will display some facts about the trail, weather conditions, Indians, mountains and all the dangers the journey possesses. You will have to slosh through mud, walk in dust six inches deep and cross swollen rivers. Your party will run short of supplies and will have to hunt and trade to replenish them. In each case you must make decisions that will affect your life or may cause your death and the deaths of your companions.

After learning about the trail, begin your journey by typing **1,** for **Travel the Trail**, and pressing <Enter>.

The first question the program asks is who you want to be, a banker from Boston, a carpenter or a farmer. Find out the differences in these professions by entering the number **6** for more information. But in your own mind, you would know that the banker would have the most money and the farmer might have the most difficult time of it.

Next, select your traveling companions. The program asks for your name, as the leader, and the five stalwart comrades who are going to travel with you. After typing in the names and checking them, continue.

Buy your supplies. You're given a certain amount of money and clues as to what to buy. This introduces the concept of budgeting. Save some money for emergency supplies and for hiring help to cross the rivers. You can also buy supplies at forts along the way; but it is much more expensive to buy on the trail than in town.

Now decide when to start on the trail. If you start too early in the year, you will run into winter snowstorms and blizzards at the beginning. If you leave too late, and survive the trip, you will run into the same bad weather near the end of your journey. Thus you learn how important timing is in decision making, and how you must consider factors that are beyond your control.

At this point, you can always access the general screen which looks like this:

The Oregon Trail

****

You may ..

1. Continue on Trail
2. Check Supplies
3. Look at Map
4. Change Pace
5. Change Food Rations
6. Stop to Rest
7. Attempt to Trade
8. Hunt for food

****

Each of these selections should be used so you are familiar with them and know en and how to use them.

During the trip, you must decide how to cross the many rivers based on the width and the th of the water. Watch the amount of food you have left and reduce the daily rations **(5)** if run low on food.

As food runs short, you will go hunting **(8)**.

Check your maps **(3)** to see how far you have gone and make a decision on alternate routes.

Trade supplies **(7)** when you are short of food and do not have many bullets for hunting.

There are a number of sick people in the wagon. You may decide to rest **(6)** because, haps, that will help them recover. But each day of rest means using up more supplies without making any progress on your journey.

When hunting (**8**) sometimes there is an abundance of game and sometimes almost none. The first time, you shoot a lot of game only to find out that you can't carry all of it back to the wagon. After that, you learn to shoot only the game you need.

By talking to other people, you find there is a delay to get the ferry and decide to go across the river in a different way.

As you travel the Oregon Trail, you learn to get information, make decisions and carry out actions. Too many wrong decisions and you die on the plains or in the mountains. Fortunately, unlike the real settlers, you can start the game over and make better decisions the next time.

For the Parent

Where in the US is Carmen Sandiego ?
Where in the World is Carmen Sandiego ?
                      &
Where in America's past is Carmen Sandiego ?

These three games will help students learn history, geography and current events. These programs will also enhance cultural literacy. To be culturally literate is to possess the basic information needed to thrive in the modern world. Information about the world is essential to the development of reading and writing skills. A person cannot understand newspaper stories without knowing where Hong Kong, Yugoslavia, Australia, Japan, Guatemala, Jerusalem or Berlin are on the globe and their relative importance in the scheme of things. This is the basic background information that every informed individual needs.

To understand what is happening in the U.S. today, one needs to know something about our nation's history. Understanding America's past will give anyone a better perspective on current events. *Where in America's past is Carmen Sandiego?* helps address the historical knowledge gap showing up in recent surveys. A Gallup poll found that almost half of current college seniors do not know when the American Civil War was fought. A quarter of the college seniors didn't even know when Columbus discovered America.

The power of playing an interactive teaching game, compared to passively listening to a lecture or watching television, cannot be overemphasized. Douglas Davis, one of the television critics for the *New York Times* found this out recently by watching a little drama unfold in his own home. PBS now has a television program modeled after the *Carmen Sandiego* educational computer games. Mr. Davis turned on the program so his children could watch it, then sat down at his computer. Soon his children were at his side demanding: ``We want the real Carmen Sandiego!''

Within a few minutes the kids were glued to the computer screen and lost to the outside world. The television was still on, but the kids were interested in the computer game in which *Carmen's* treacherous colleagues had purloined the original manuscript of Shakespeare's *Macbeth*. On the television, three students played a version of the Carmen game quizzed by hosts Greg Lee and Lynne Thigpig. Questions cover geography, history and art. The show is a wonderful step up from normal kiddy fare. But for the Davis children, the real thing was the interactive computer version of *Carmen*. When kids sit down at their PC, *Carmen* commands their full attention and demands literacy in a way that no educational television show can duplicate. Mr. Davis concluded: ``Television as we know it, pales beside any interactive computer program ....''

The use of television combined with a computer will be the next step in interactive educational technology. Some preliminary developments have been shown, but the real interactive concept, along with the corresponding software, has not yet been developed. Until such powerful multi-media programs are developed, *Carmen Sandiego* on a PC provides one of the most exciting learning experiences for children.

For the Student

What Is *Carmen Sandiego?*

Where in the World is Carmen Sandiego?

There are a strange bunch of thieves loose in the world and they're stealing treasures all over the globe. As a detective it is your job to find and arrest the criminals.

After working with **Carmen Sandiego?** you'll be able to:

1. Look for information (research).

Compile information by putting together the clues until you can identify the suspect, (using research material).

2. Look at clues that lead you further (expanding information base).

3. Look up important facts, (reference lookup).

4. Prepare a warrant (paperwork) to capture the villain.

While playing **Carmen**, you learn about geography, economics, history, language and facts relating to the countries of the world while developing your deductive reasoning skills.

In this version, the thieves steal historical treasures such as Ben Franklin's kite, the Statue of Liberty, and the Declaration of Independence. *Where in America's past is Carmen Sandiego?* covers 400 years of U.S. history. The object of the game is to capture the thieves as they travel across the country and through time. The software comes with a book *(What Happened When: A Chronology of Life and Events in America)* that lets you look up special events and find the time period and location where the thieves are hiding.

For example; you are given a clue: "She said she was going down South to re-enact Huckleberry Finn's trip down the Mississippi." With that clue you go to the Chronoskimmer time machine which takes you to the Mississippi of Mark Twain's time. If the vile henchman you are looking for is not there, bystanders will say they haven't seen anyone of that description. If you are in the right place and time, you will see the henchman slink across the screen. You know you're hot on the trail. You can get another clue from a bystander and move on in pursuit.

Starting the program

After you start the program from the Menu and press **G** for game the program will ask you to identify yourself. Type in your name and, as this is the first time you have played the game, it assigns you a Detective Status -- Rookie.

It will then tell you that a treasure has been stolen from _____ .

Example: Cairo.

In the process, it will tell you about the treasure and mention some historical information.

If you don't know where the city is, look it up in the Almanac. As you continue, the program gives the first clue about your suspect.

A man was seen fleeing from the Museum with a treasure. (Clue: male).

You are given a time period during which you must catch him. There are four keys you can access for help.

1. See   **2. Depart**   **3. Clue**   **4. Crime**

The clue (**3**) gives three places to gather information by going and asking questions.

You may visit a museum, library, hotel or marketplace. At the hotel the desk clerk gives you a clue to where the criminal is headed. "He asked if the dollar had dropped." This gives you the clue that he is probably headed to the U.S. However, there are other countries such as Canada that also use the dollar. You may want to go for another clue. This time you walk to the library and the librarian says, for example, that the suspect wanted a book on skyscrapers.

Once you have a clue (or some clues) that leads you to the next city, use them to find the place the suspect is going.

By typing (**1**) for See, you find that one of the cities is New York. With the two clues -- dollars and skyscrapers -- it seems a likely choice.

Type (**2**) for Depart and click New York, or move the lightbar down to NY and press <Enter> on the keyboard. The time clock clicks away the hours of flying time until you get to your destination. You then proceed to get the next clue. If you have gone to the wrong location bystanders will say: "I have seen no one with that description." In this location you might get two more clues about the suspect. One person says he saw him and he had red hair. Another says he was trying to hide a tattoo. At this point, move to Compute. Moving to each characteristic, flip through it until you find the right match: male, red hair, tattoo. Then ask to compute. If the characteristics determine a unique individual, then a warrant for his arrest can be issued and you know you are close.

Continue following the clues. As you get closer there are a number of attempts to knock you off. However, you finally capture the thief (if you don't run out of time) and are asked one more question to look up in the almanac. Answer correctly and you are promoted.

Example: "What was the book that started the environmental movement?" Answer: *The Silent Spring* by Rachel Carson.

After you have answered the question correctly, continue on to a new case. The cases get harder as you go along.

By playing this game you learn about different aspects of many countries: the mountains of Nepal, the pyramids of Egypt, the rivers of Brazil, the type of money used in India.

Many things you learn in **Oregon Trail** and **Carmen Sandiego** can be useful to you in school and in life, but the most important part is to learn how to make decisions while traveling the trail or capturing **Carmen.**

For the Parent

Math Blaster Mystery

Although a math program, *Math Blaster Mystery* has a far wider range of educational concepts connected to it than the other math programs in the **Computer Curriculum**. It therefore fits better with **Decision Making** software. *Math Blaster Mystery* was designed to stimulate higher-order thinking skills and strategies for solving problems. It is particularly successful in meeting the needs of problem solving situations and applications requiring detailed analysis. Along with the process of getting students thinking, it is a motivating and fun game that challenges them at many different levels.

The most challenging math problems that students face, in the classroom or on college placement tests, are word problems. These types of problems are closer to the problems your student will face in real life than most other types of math problems. The world would be much easier if it presented us with all problems in neat mathematical formulas, but, unfortunately, we are often presented with a situation that calls for analysis before we can decide the mathematical aspect of the problem. *MBM (Math Blaster Mystery)* enhances students' abilities to analyze and reformulate problems into mathematical equations.

1. Follow the Steps

Follow the Steps is the first activity in **Math Blaster Mystery**. It contains word problems to challenge the student, not only in finding the answer but also in deciding what steps are needed to solve the problem. The student is taught to read the problem carefully, analyze it and start down the path to solving it. Each step is an integral part of the process from finding out what the real question is to deciding what facts are necessary to solve the problem.

The student must identify relevant, and discard superfluous information to solve the problem. Feedback is provided along each step so the student learns how logic can be applied and understands if s/he has made a misstep. After the logic has been applied, the problem then asks the student to find the correct mathematical expression of the problem and to use this formula to solve it.

Follow the Steps has four levels of difficulty determined by a combination of the number of steps involved and the type of mathematics used. The easier problems contain two steps using addition and subtraction, multiplication and division of whole numbers.

The more difficult problems contain three steps involving percentages, decimals and fractions used in different combinations.

The entire process is tremendously challenging and teaches your child in a way that is difficult to replicate even in the classroom.

2. Weigh the Evidence

Weigh the Evidence, compels students to develop strategies for moving a set of weights from one scale to another. Students must analyzing the problem to find out which weights are needed for the solution, breaking the problem into smaller steps to approach the solution. Students must also think ahead to plan an effective strategy for dealing with spatial relations. The four levels in this activity start with whole numbers and continue to fractions, decimals and percentages. Thinking ability and understanding of spatial relationships are developed by this program as well as teaching multiple step solutions to problems.

3. Decipher the Code

Decipher the Code challenges the student to make inferences and draw conclusions from numerical information. It helps the student develop higher order thinking skills while learning to develop hypotheses and test them. The student also gets to test and use alternative strategies to solve the mystery.

4. Search for Clues

Search for Clues is a game in which students find a mystery number by searching for clues in a room full of objects and characters. Interpreting the clues challenges students to learn many ways to describe and define a number. Many mathematical concepts are effectively reinforced by making students apply their knowledge of math and terminology to reasoning with numbers. Students learn to organize information, make inferences and draw conclusions. Their deductive and inductive reasoning skills are developed.

For the Student

Starting *Math Blaster Mystery*

To start the program:

> 1. Move the lightbar on the *menu* to **Math Blaster Mystery**
> Press <Enter>.

The screen asks for your name. It is important that you type in your name the same way each time so that record keeping will be consistent.

> 1. Type in your name: (up to 20 letters)

> 2. Press <Enter> or click OK with your mouse.

The program asks for the date, which is also needed for accurate record keeping. If your computer has a calendar in it you need only press <Enter> or click OK. If not, use the arrow keys to get the correct date. You can move between the boxes by using the <Tab> key. When the date is displayed correctly, press <Enter> or click OK.

The Davidson Student Desktop Interface then comes to the screen.

Before beginning the activities complete the following set-up procedures at this menu:

1. On the F2 menu (FILE) move the lightbar down to **record keeping** and press <Enter>.

This will select record keeping.

2. Use the arrow keys or the mouse to move to the **subject** menu.

3. Move the lightbar to the correct place and click the mouse or press <Enter>.

4. Use the arrow keys to move to LEVEL and, based upon your starting point test, move the arrow down to the proper level and press <Enter>.

Only two more steps and you are ready to start the program.
First we must set up your file for record keeping.

5. Press F2 or click with the mouse to bring down the file menu.

6 Set up a record keeping file as you did with MATH BLASTER PLUS. See Chapter. 9.

1. TO FOLLOW THE STEPS:

1. Using the arrow keys, move around the menu screen to **Follow the Steps**. Press <Enter>.

Begin with the following steps:

1. What does the problem ask you to find? This requires reading the problem carefully and fully understanding what you have to do. After you have selected the correct answer, the problem will be highlighted. This step is the key to all word problems.

2. What information is needed to solve the problem? This step asks you for the facts needed to solve the equation. This is an extemely important part of problem solving or setting up experiments. What information is needed and what is unnecessary information. After you answer this, the key facts willl be underlined in the problem.

3. Once you know what the facts are, it is time to write a mathematical expression representing the calculation necessary to reach the solution. In order to accomplish this, you must really understand the problem.

4. The last step is to calculate the answer. (The software has a built in calculator. To bring it to the screen press <Esc> and move to **file.** Pull down the menu and click **calculator**). You can operate the calculator in two ways:

1. Enter the numbers from the keyboard and type in the =, \ , + or - signs.

· Or

2. Click on the numbers to get the answer.

2. WEIGH THE EVIDENCE:

Using the arrow keys move around the menu screen to **Weigh the Evidence** and press <Enter>.

Example:

1. There are four weights on scale A: 92, 13, 40, 44 lbs.

2. At the top of the screen is a target number: e.g. 97.

3. Determine which weights will make up that number (in this case 44, 40, 13).

4. Determine which weight is not needed (in this case 92).

5. Move the weights from scale A to another scale (B or C).

NOTE: Heavier weights cannot be put on top of lighter ones.

6. Move the weights back and forth until you have the correct stack -- an amount that adds up to the target number, on scale B or C.

The object is to do this in the minimum number of moves possible.

3. DECIPHER THE CODE:

Using the arrow keys move around the menu screen to **Decipher the Code** and press < Enter > .

1. Enter a series of numbers/signs in a row of boxes to form an equation. When you press < Enter > the clues are given.

2. If a number or sign is in the correct position it will be carried up to the next row.

3. If a number or sign is used in the equation, but is not in the correct position, it will remain white.

4. A number or sign not in the equation at all will also remain white.

5. On the right hand side of the screen is a notepad with numbers. If a number has not yet been tried or placed in its correct position it too remains white.

6. Black boxes contain numbers/signs that should no longer be used

171

4. SEARCH FOR CLUES

Using the arrow keys, move around the menu screen to **Search for Clues** and press <Enter>.

1. With the mouse, select an object in the room and click it .

2. A clue is revealed. (Example: n is a factor of 15.)

3. Enter a logical guess. (Example: guess 5.) That's logical but not correct. You may enter more clues. Example guess: 4. 4 is not logical because it is not a factor of 15. In this case an arrow will point to the conflicting clue and you may try another guess.

You will get a score based upon the number of tries it took you to achieve the correct answer. You can get assistance by using the **help screen** to view definitions of formulas or information supplied by the clues.

Summary

This program fits into the decision making and problem solving portion of the **Computer Curriculum.** In the first activity, the student analyzes problems and formulates ways to find answers. In the second activity, students deal with strategies and problem solving and, in the final section, they get *clues* that force them to use deductive reasoning to solve problems.

Chapter 12

Typing, Writing and Desktop Publishing

For the Parent or Teacher

Why Typing Is Important for Students

 Imagine you are living early in the 19th century. Rubbing your cramped hands, you contemplate writing the tenth letter of the evening. It's taken three hours, your pen nib is worn, the ink is beginning to clot, but you know you must continue.

It was not until 1872 that an inventor by the name of S.W. Soule developed a machine that could write faster than anyone could by pen. However, it had tremendous problems with the keys jamming. Finally, in desperation, Soule took a step that has had a profound effect on the whole world. Since he couldn't redesign the machine to work faster, he redesigned the keyboard to force the typist to type slower. He perfected the awkward QWERTY keyboard which we are stuck with today.

Since the invention of the typewriter, the typed word has become an intrinsic part of how the world operates. Our world is composed of typewritten documents, from the newspaper we read to the memo's and resumes we write.

What the typewriter was to the world in the 19th century the computer is today. However, to use this modern machine, one must learn the antiquated keyboard of the 1800's.

Mavis Beacon Teaches Typing

This typing program has all of the capabilities of an interactive program with artificial intelligence. It has excellent graphics to engage the student's attention and keeps track of the number and types of mistakes a student makes, as well as lessons in which the student requires the most practice. *Mavis Beacon Teaches Typing* meets all of the requirements for a good educational program. As in all of the recommended educational software this program has multiple approaches to teaching the subject.

The Chalkboard

In any good classroom, the teacher puts the assignment on the chalkboard. Students remember their assignment better if they see the information in a written form. Mavis does the same before each lesson. The teaching plan is on the chalkboard, which appears on the screen.

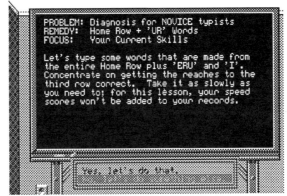

Each lesson emphasizes a particular aspect of typing: new letters of the alphabet, speed of typing, rhythm or dropped characters. Mavis has taught many students and she knows which are the best lessons for each. The chalkboard tells the student what particular aspect of typing to practice.

The Classroom

The classroom screen looks like a computer, complete with monitor and keyboard. The keyboard shows all of the letters while a pair of guided hands show correct finger placement. As you are given a letter to practice, the fingers on the screen move as well, demonstrating *touch typing*, i.e. typing without looking at the keyboard. A student's typing will often consist of copying a document or typing something out of a book. To maintain speed it is important to keep an eye on the book while typing. Touch typing, while difficult at first, will eventually become second nature, allowing the student to maintain a good typing speed. As each key is depressed, the screen lights up. The on-screen keys can be used to help develop touch typing. Students should look at the monitor as they type, not the keyboard. The on-screen keys will help increase speed and accuracy.

The Workshop

This screen is used to develop students' ability to maintain a good rhythm in typing, giving immediate feedback on speed and accuracy. It also shows the keys and finger placement, as does the Classroom screen. A metronome helps develop a steady method of typing.

Studies have shown that use of a steady beat helps new typists increase their typing speed. When first learning to type, a new typist will tend to pause before going for a difficult finger reach such as *q* or *p,* causing fingers to falter. Using the beat of the metronome helps to overcome this problem.

The Arcade

Mavis presents a special challenge for students who have learned the first lesson. Placed in the cockpit of a high-performance race car students must type the way to victory. It's just like in an arcade game, but all the while students will be learning to type. Pitted against "Red Walter", who likes nothing better than to leave competitors in the dust, students must type quickly to leave "Red" fading in the rear view mirror. Slow down and he starts to creep up. If the student makes a typing mistake, a bug splatters on the windshield. With too many mistakes, the windshield becomes bug splattered, leaving little visibility. Some students have wiped out the entire bug population of their state. While dangerous to insects, this game is a great way to increase both speed and accuracy.

FOR THE STUDENT

Starting the Program

1. Move the lightbar to **Mavis** and press < Enter > . The basic Mavis program screen appears.

2. The first time you do this, move the light bar to the **Meet Mavis** program and press < Enter > . This will walk you through the various programs.

There is also an explanation for the New User.

3. Move the lightbar to **New User**, press < Enter > and read the brief explanation.

You are ready to start the lesson.

Beginning a Lesson

1. Move the lightbar to **Start Lesson** and press < Enter > .

2. Press < Enter > and type in your name using the hunt and peck mode for the last time. Press < Enter > and input your last name. Press < Enter > .

3. Move the lightbar to **Beginner** and press < Enter > .

Even if you have had previous typing experience, I would recommend that you start the program as a beginner

4. Move the bar to your age group and press < Enter > .

5.   When the screen asks if everything is correct move the bar to **I want to change something** and press <Enter>.

6.   Move the light bar to **time limit** and use the right and left arrows to change it. Set your time limit to 30 minutes. That is a good practice segment. At the end of that time period, the program will ask you if you want to continue.

7. Press <Esc> and the parameters of your age and the time period for a practice session will be set.

8. The lightbar will be at **Yes let's do that**   press <Enter> to get started.

The first exercise covers the *a s d f* keys. It is important that you start off with ɔod habits.   Do not look at the keyboard. At the end of the first lesson, if you made ɹistakes, the program will ask if you want to repeat the lesson. It is a good idea to repeat for additional practice.

When the lesson is completed, the computer will ask if you want to continue or to ɔ something else. I recommend that you continue. But, let's first take a look at the ternatives.

ɐts play a game	This will activate the arcade game.
ɐke another suggestion	This suggests an alternative lesson.
ɐpeat the last lesson	Even though you may not have made many mistakes you may want to repeat a lesson for additional practice.
F7> How am I doing	This will present charts showing your speed and accuracy on all the different keys.
F10> Quit the program	This will allow you to delete a user, or to quit the program.

ɔu can either push the function key listed beside the command or if no function keys are ɐted move the lightbar to the command and press <Enter>.

Continuing the Program

If you choose to continue, the program will start you on actual typing. As you only know four letters at this time, the words you type will not be very meaningful. By the time you finish this program, however, you will be typing letters and reports.

At the end of typing your first set of words, the program will tell you if you beat your target speed and ask if you want to increase it. The basic target speed is 20 wpm. The program will tell you your actual speed and accuracy.

The first four segments of the typing program work with the home keys, the basis for all touch typing. After exhausting the specific keys, the practice begins using words.

Repeating for Practice

1. If after doing an exercises you feel that you still need more practice; go to the chalkboard, move the lightbar to **Lets do something else** and press <Enter>.
2. Move the lightbar to **Repeat the last lesson** and press <Enter>.
This will give you a chance to practice that lesson again.

The Metronome

The metronome exercise will help develop a rhythm for your typing. To change the speed of the metronome, consult you Mavis manual or press **F1** for help. If you are taking music lessons this section will be familiar to you.

The Road Race

This section of the program lets you focus on speed, but you must still maintain you accuracy. It's also a lot of fun to splatter bugs on the windshield when you make mistakes. The letters you actually typed show in the instrument panel while your typing speed shows in the speedometer.

Finishing a Lesson

After you have finished the planned lessons for the day, or the computer program has indicated that it is the end of your time period, go to the **What to do next** menu.

1. Move the lightbar to **Show Graphs of Progress** and look at your **Adjusted Words Per Minute** by session.

2. Move lightbar to **Show Graph**.

Look at your Problem keys.

3. Move the lightbar to **Exit From Graphs** and press < Enter >.

Continuing with MAVIS

It is important that you practice typing during the first three months of this curriculum. In order to use word processing to write letters and reports you need a good foundation in typing. The typing is broken down into segments and after each segment here is a report on speed and accuracy. At the end of each session, you should print out a report which shows your current speed and accuracy. The first level to aim for is a speed of 10 words per minute with a minimum of 85% accuracy.
The report looks like this.

Typist's Report Card
Today's overall adjusted Words per Minute Score: 12
Previous Session Scores
Date: 5/5/92   Exercises done 3   Adj. Words per minute 9
Date: 5/2/92   Exercises done 2   Adj. Words per minute 6

Post these numbers to the progress chart in appendix C, which will show your progress during the period. Even after the first three months, you should still come back to **Mavis** at various points to practice and improve your typing.

ONCE UPON A TIME

For the Parent

Elaborate crayon drawings hang on the refrigerators of parents across the United States (and perhaps the world). Perhaps this colorful form of art has graced your favorite kitchen appliance as well. While most adults might see a house, cow, or simply squiggly lines in these drawings, the children who have rendered them will undoubtedly be able to provide a rich and complex story to explain the scene depicted. Unfortunately, the imagination displayed in such stories seems to disappear as our children enter elementary school. *Once Upon A Time* can rekindle this imagination by allowing children to create stores based upon the pictures they draw.

This program starts by bringing a *background* on the screen. In Volume 1 of this program (there are three volumes available) the possible backgrounds are **Main Street, Farm, or Safari.** Once the background has been put on the screen, the student can place other objects into the story. This program develops the concept of story creation and illustration. With *Once Upon a Time* writing becomes an exciting adventure.

For the Student

Starting the Program

To start the program move the lightbar to *Once Upon a Time* on the menu and press < Enter > .

Choose the correct video, **CGA, EGA** or **VGA** display mode and press <Enter>. Usually the selection that the program recommends will be the correct one.

> **CGA**
> **TANDY**
> **MCGA**
> **EGA/VGA**

An introduction screen will appear. After music, a screen called *Passport to Discovery* will display.

1. Use the arrow keys to select **Safari** and press <Enter>.

2. Move the lightbar to **Draw** and press <Enter>, (It may already be at Draw.)

3. Press <**F1**> to display a list of objects you can put in the picture.

4. Move the lightbar down to **alligator.** (If you press F2 it will sound the word.)

5. Type in the name of the object **alligator.** (This program will not let you select an object by moving the lightbar.)

The program will ask where to put the alligator.

6. You can move the alligator by using the arrows. When you have put it where you want, press <Enter>.

7. Move the lightbar to **New background** and press <Enter>. A new background will appear.
(Each story has four different backgrounds.) (We will use the second background for this session.)

8. Move the lightbar to **Flip** and press < Enter >. It will ask you to type the name of the object you want to flip. Type **jeep** and press < Enter >. The jeep is now facing in the other direction.

9. Use the arrow keys to highlight **Write-Edit** and press < Enter >.

Write a story about the picture, using whatever comes into your mind. Be silly or serious. Don't worry if what you are writing makes sense. Write your ideas down as quickly as possible without stopping to think about them. A proven technique for unlocking imaginative powers, free flow writing is how famous writers like *Ray Bradbury* come up with their most creative stories. Once you have written a story, you can go back and make changes but, for now, just let the ideas flow from your head to your fingers and onto the computer keyboard. (Don't worry about what happens when you reach the end of the line. The program will automatically start a new line for you.)

10. When you finish writing the picture caption press < Esc >.

Use the arrow keys to highlight **Next page** and press < Enter >.

11. The program will ask **What is the name of the New Book?**
Type in a name (e.g. jungle). This is the file name. It cannot exceed 8 characters.

12. The program will ask **Picture** or **Text.** Highlight **Text** and press < Enter >. A new page will appear.

13. Press < **F9** > and read the edit features, then press any key to return to the text page.

14. Press < Esc > to return to the page. When you have finished your story press < Esc > to return to the picture/menu. If you have another page, highlight **Text** and press < Enter >.

Titling and Saving Your Story

1. Using the arrow keys move the highlight to **Edit Book.**

2. Press <**F1**> and type the title. Press <Esc>.

3. Press <**F2**> and type your name. Press <Esc>.

4. Check that everything appears correct then press <Esc>.

5. At the end of the story use the arrow keys to highlight **Save book** and press <Enter>. Each page of the story will be saved as a book.

Printing Your Story

1. Use the arrow keys to highlight **Print** and press <Enter>. The printer name will be displayed on the screen.

Options: **Print Page**
       Print Book
       New Printer
       Quit

2. If this is the first time you have printed a story, use the arrow keys to highlight **New Printer** and press <Enter>.

3. A list of printers will be displayed. Use the arrow keys to highlight your printer and press <Enter>.

4. Highlight print and press <Enter>. Your book will now print.

The New Print Shop

What Is Desktop Publishing?

From the invention of the first printing press until the advent of desktop publishing about 10 years ago, creating a publication required many people with different skills. For a newsletter, a writer would type up the stories, a professional typesetter would set them in neat columns, a graphic artist would hand draw cartoons, charts and other ``graphics'' to illustrate the articles and a designer would draw a rough sketch to show where the articles and graphics should go on the newsletter pages. Finally, a paste-up person would take typeset articles and illustrations and physically glue them onto blank pages following that rough sketch. Desktop publishing software lets you do all these things by yourself, electronically. You write the stories, set them into type, select cartoons and charts and then put it all together, like pieces of a puzzle, on your computer screen. You can print out complete newsletter pages, ready to be copied and distributed. No pasting or struggling with T-squares; you do it all on your computer. Desktop publishing puts the power of the press into the hands of anyone who owns a personal computer and printer. With *The New Print Shop* you, too, can become a creative writer, designer and publisher.

For Parents and Students

Pencil and paper are productivity tools. *Microsoft Works* is a writing productivity tool. *Once Upon a Time* is a creative productivity tool. *The New Print shop* is a graphic art creative productivity tool. It is one of the exciting new types of software to emerge in the past few years. It has the ability to combine text (words) with computer graphics (pictures) to produce ready-to-print publications including newsletters, reports and books as well as fun things like personalized greeting cards and signs. This program can open a whole new world of communication for you.

Vocabulary for Print Shop

The words listed below are vocabulary you should be familiar with in order to understand **Desktop Publishing** and *Print Shop*. You will find these terms commonly used in all desktop publishing software programs.

graphics: cartoons and charts designs and illustrations, as opposed to written words.

clip-art: Illustrations or graphics that can be inserted into a publication on the computer. For example, if you were writing a report about building a better mousetrap, you might use a clip art illustration of a mouse.

print font: A style of printed letters and numbers. For example, the letters you are reading now are from a font called Times Roman. The New York Times newspaper is printed in this font, ergo its name.

printer setup: Setting the software in the computer so that the document you create on the screen will come out accurately on your printer.

import: To bring in text or graphics from another application. For example, if you were doing a report on the economy you might want to include a chart someone else in your family created using the LOTUS 1-2-3 spreadsheet software. To electronically copy that graphics file into your report, you would import it.

For the Student

The New Print Shop

This program has a split screen which allows you to see the menu options and view the publication you're creating at the same time. It is one of the easiest programs to learn and use. If you follow the key steps in the beginning of the program you will have many hours of fun creating greeting cards, calendars and your own newsletter or school newspaper. The program offers more than 100 clip-art graphics and gives you the capability to import others. Multiple graphics can be placed anywhere on a page then moved, re-sized, flipped or centered. There are ten different print fonts along with a combination of style options. Some examples are:

Happy   *Happy*   Happy   Happy   *Happy*   **Happy**

Different fonts in a variety of sizes can be used on a single page.
The program also includes many ready-made signs, banners and certificates that are very helpful in learning how to use the program, and fun as well.

In addition to fonts, the program has a variety of illustrations in clip-art. These pictures, a birthday cake for example, can be used to enhance any of your projects. As you get more involved in desktop publishing, you may want to buy additional clip-art. Broderbund (the company that makes *The New Print Shop*) offers sets of illustrations for business and school as well as a party collection.

tarting Print Shop:

1. Move the lightbar on the menu to ***NEW PRINT SHOP*** and press <Enter>.

Menu Screen:

```
                    THE PRINT SHOP
************************************************************
     MAIN MENU                          PREVIEW
************************************************************
     Greeting Card
     Sign or Poster
     Letterhead
     Banner
     Calendar
     Name file
     Quick Print
     Graphic Editor
     Setup
     Exit
************************************************************
ress Enter to select      Esc to Exit      F1 = Help
```

1. Move the lightbar to **Setup** and press <Enter>.

2. Move the lightbar to **Select Printer** and press <Enter>.

3. Use the arrow keys to move the lightbar to your printer's name, e.g. **Hewlett Packard Deskjet** (If you can't find the model name for your printer check your printer manual for an equivalent.)

4. Press <Enter> to **Confirm Your Selection.**

5. Move the lightbar to **Test Printer** and press <Enter>.

6. Move the lightbar to **Save Setup**. Press <Enter>

NOTE: Step 6 is very important. If you do not save the setup you will have to repeat these steps the next time you use *Print Shop*.

Greeting Card:

To get familiar with the program, lets go through the steps to create a simple birthday card. Our next project will be more complex and utilize many more of the features of *PRINT SHOP*.

1. Move light bar to **Greeting Card** and press <Enter>

2. Move lightbar to **Design Your Own** press <Enter>

3. Move to **Side Fold Card** and press <Enter>.

Project Menu:

You are in the Project Menu. The screen on the right side is the preview screen. On the left is the selection screen (in this case the menu for the front of the card). This is the key screen for selecting what you want to do.

1. Highlight **Border** and press <Enter>.

2. Select the **Thin** file and press <Enter>.

3. Using the arrow move the lightbar to **Neon** press <Enter>.

NOTE: As you move the lightbar through the borders an example of each is displayed in the preview window.

Once you have selected a border, the preview window will display it.

4. On the left Front Menu move the lightbar to **Graphic** and press <Enter>.

5. Using the arrow keys, scroll down until you find a design you like, then press <Enter>.

The Graphics are now displayed in the preview window. In the **Change Graphics** window there is a message as to how to change the graphic.

To clear a space in the graphic to print a message.

1. Use the arrow key until the graphic in the center is outlined. This is the area you will want to use to write your message.

2. Press the <Spacebar> to delete that graphic.

3. Press <Enter> to indicate that you have selected the balance of the graphic.

4. Move the lightbar in the Front Menu to **Message** and press <Enter>.

5. Move the lightbar to **Sonoma** font and press <Enter>.

6. Move the lightbar to **Solid Style** and press <Enter>.

7. Type *Happy* and press <Enter>.

8. Type *Birthday* and press <Enter>.

9. Type *Fred* (or any other name) but DO NOT press the enter key.

10. Press the <**F8**> function key to center the message.

11. Press <F10> for a preview to see how the card will look.

Note: **PRINT SHOP** does not have a good text editor. In order to make changes you need to backspace (erasing all text) and then retype.

12. Press <Esc> at the point when you have finished entering the text.

13. The preview part of the screen will display the front of the card.

14. The lightbar is now on the **Inside of Card**. Press <Enter> to select.

Creating the inside of a greeting card:

Selecting a border:

1. Move the lightbar to **border** press <Enter>

2. Highlight **Wide** and press <Enter>.

3. Highlight **Balloons** and press <Enter>.

The preview window displays the selected border.

Specifying the graphics:

1. Highlight **Graphics** (clipart) and press <Enter>.

2. Move lightbar to **Small Corner Placement** and press <Enter>.

3. Move lightbar to **Graphics File** and press <Enter>.

4. Move lightbar to **Ice Cream** and press <Enter>.

5. An Ice Cream cone will appear in the corner of the card.

To Change some of the graphics:

1. Use the arrow keys to highlight the **graphic** in the lower left corner.

2. Press <C> to change the graphic. A list of graphics appears in the window.

3. Move the lightbar to the **Cake Slice Graphic** and press <Enter>.

4. The Cake Slice replaces the Ice Cream graphic.

Enter the Message:

1. Highlight **Message** and press <Enter>.

2. Move the lightbar to **Ventura Font.**

3. Move the lightbar to **Outline** type style.

4. Type **It's Time** and press <Enter>.

5. Type **to** and press <Enter>.

6. Type **Celebrate** but *DO NOT* press the enter key.

7. Press <F8> to center the message.

8. Press <Esc> to return to the menu.

You have now completed an invitation. Although there are many features to ``customize'' the card to be more creative with it, save and print your card so that you can see the result of your work.

Save the card:

1. Highlight **Save Design** on the inside menu and press <Enter>.

2. Type in a title such as **Birth1,** and press <Enter>.

This design is now saved and can be used at a later time or you can change it for other people (change name) or different themes.

Print the card:

1. Move the lightbar to **Test Paper Position** and press <Enter>.

2. The printer will print a row of dots which should run directly over the horizontal perforations. When printing graphics, position is very important, testing the paper position this will let you print a perfect card. (If you have a laser printer this is not necessary.)

3. If the paper is not properly aligned, move it and repeat the process until it is.

4. Move the lightbar to **Print** and press <Enter>

The greeting card is now printed. See the sample that is enclosed in your software box to see how to fold it properly. You have now completed your first project using *Print Shop.* I will briefly outline one more exercise to give you the feel of another type of project but, after that, a review of the print shop manual will expand your horizons for the capabilities of the program.

Calendar

With *Print Shop* you can create daily, weekly and monthly calendars. Let's create a ``Homework'' calendar to keep track of assignments.

Creating the Calendar:

Begin working with **Calendar** by selecting it from the menu the way you did with **Card**. Check the *Print Shop* manual if you have specific questions about the procedure for **Calendar**.

The calendar has three parts, top, middle and bottom. You begin by designing the top. On it you select graphics the same way you did in the other project. Select **Books** because this is a school project.

1 9 9 3

Enter the time period, such as Sept. 5-12, and put down the subjects you are currently taking in school. Create the calendar one month in advance.

If your calendar is a weekly calendar it will appear as follows.

Sunday Sept. 5
Monday Sept. 6

A monthly calendar will have a box for each day. You would enter your schedule in each date box.

After putting in your school week, schedule your **Computer Curriculum** and any projects you have coming up. This should include not only the completion date of the project but also the start work date and progress steps.

For Example: If a book report is due Nov. 15, schedule the reading of the book to start Nov. 1, to be read by Nov. 10. A first draft of the report should be complete on Nov. 11 and the final report completed by Nov. 14.

This will help organize your schoolwork.

Summary

These two examples give you an idea of some uses for *The   Print Shop* program. As you work with the software you will learn to be more creative and find that you have a wonderful tool for communicating. If you catch the publishing bug and want to do more sophisticated work, *Print Shop* will have set the ground work for you to move into more complex **Desktop Publishing.** You'll be ready to join the communications revolution of the 21st century.

Chapter 13

Word Processing with Microsoft Works

For Parents and Students

A Brief History of Writing

> *"To know how to write well is to know how to think well"*
> **Pascal**

 Almost twenty-two thousand years ago, in cave paintings at Lascaux, the first pictures were produced. It was another seventeen millennia before human kind's most extraordinary achievement, the art of writing, made its appearance. The first instrument for writing was the stone chisel. Letters and symbols were cut into stone. Not only was this form of writing tedious, but if the "writer" made a mistake, he had to throw the stone away and start over.

The next stage of writing was scratching letters into wet clay, creating clay tablets. The Sumerians used them for recording the number of sacks of grain, heads of cattle and other agricultural resources. The clay was easier to write on because one could scratch letters into wet clay with a stick. Errors could simply be wiped away. However, if the writer found a mistake after the tablet was baked and hardened, it was necessary to throw it away and create a new one.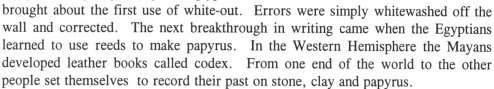

Stone and clay tablets were replaced when the Egyptians began painting hieroglyphics on walls. This brought about the first use of white-out. Errors were simply whitewashed off the wall and corrected. The next breakthrough in writing came when the Egyptians learned to use reeds to make papyrus. In the Western Hemisphere the Mayans developed leather books called codex. From one end of the world to the other people set themselves to record their past on stone, clay and papyrus.

Three thousand years ago the alphabet was invented. It was not an instantaneous event but the result of a long history of development. Later, for more than a thousand years, writing skills were virtually the monopoly of monks using paper and quill. A thankless task, for if any ink was splotched the whole page had to be recopied.

John Gutenberg's printing press ushered in a revolution in book production and thus in writing. Still, the quill pen remained the indispensable tool for recording thought. Then came the lead pencil. And so someone invented that item, dear to the hearts of students everywhere, the eraser. In the 19th century, the typewriter was invented, allowing one to write quickly and legibly, fixing little mistakes with an eraser. Major goofs, however, such as putting a sentence in the wrong place, still meant starting over. Finally, in the late 20th century, the word processor was developed, allowing writers to concentrate on ideas without worrying about the difficulties of changes or corrections.

What Is a Word Processor?

A word processor is a computerized replacement for the typewriter that used to sit on the desks of almost every student and office worker. With a word processor, one can fix mistakes, rearrange text, delete words or sentences and save work on a disk as well as printing it out. In general, a word processor can do things in minutes that would require hours of work on a typewriter. The ability to quickly make changes to a document on a computer screen and print out a fresh clean copy explains why word processing programs are the number one selling software category in North America. This book was originally written in Microsoft Word for Windows and edited in WordPerfect, two of the best-selling word processing packages currently available.

An Example of Word Processing power

Here's an example of how a simple note can quickly be improved using word processing:

First Draft

Dear Sir:
Yes, I am willing trade the Aaron for a Mantle and a Drysdale. The Hank Aaron is in very fine condition. It is wrapped in plastic and has its original markings. I hope to hear from you soon and thanks for your interest in my baseball card collection.

Second Draft

Dear Sir:
Thank you for your interest in my baseball card collection.
The Hank Aaron card you inquired about is in very fine condition. It is wrapped in plastic and has its original markings. I am willing to trade it for a Mickey Mantle and a Don Drysdale. I hope to hear from you soon.

The second letter is an improvement over the first. On a typewriter, re-arranging the sentences would have required retyping the entire letter. With a word processor, sentences and words can be moved electronically before printing to create a superior letter.

Students who do their work on a word processor have a tremendous advantage in school. Writing with a pen or a typewriter can cause students to become pre-occupied with getting everything right the first time, discouraging creativity and re-writing. Meanwhile, students using word processors are free to experiment. They can write creatively off the tops of their heads because they know they can easily revise an essay or story before printing it. Even after the final paper comes out of the printer, changes can be made. Word processors routinely offer spelling checkers. Some have a thesaurus. There are even grammar checking programs available. All of these features help improve the overall quality of student papers.

There are different levels of word processing software available. Microsoft **WORKS** is a basic word processing program, but it offers capabilities that were considered advanced just a few years ago. More advanced software offers the capability of combining text with pictures and other graphics and the ability to use a variety of fonts in different sizes to produce documents that look as if they were created by a professional typesetter. With these word processing programs, the difference between word processing and desktop publishing is no longer well defined.

While it doesn't have all the capabilities of *Word for Windows* or *WordPerfect, Works* is an excellent word processor for all student. Unless they are planning to publish a book, magazine or write technical documentation, students will be happy with *Works*.

How a Word processor Is Used

A student can use word processing software to write book reports, send letters, write science projects, take notes, keep a journal or just to send messages to friends. Students who have mastered the basics of the typing program and a few word processing commands, will be able to produce documents that will make them (and probably their parents) proud.

For the Student and Parent

Definitions for Word Processing

Here are some key terms used in this section and in books and manuals about word processing.

block: A section of a document -- phrase, sentence, paragraph -- that is marked or highlighted so that it can be moved, copied or deleted.

cursor: The point or flashing marker that shows you where you are as you type and edit your document on the screen.

cut: To remove a section of the text from the document and move it to temporary storage.

paste: To place the section of the document that is in temporary storage back into the document.

delete: To remove or erase. The delete key removes to the right of the cursor. The backspace key erases (deletes) to the left.

delete section: You can delete a whole section by highlighting it and pushing the delete key.

file: A collection of information that has a specific name (not more than 8 characters).

new file: Starting a new collection of information.

name of file: The name of your document (not more than 8 characters.)

highlight: This command turns on a function that will highlight the letters as you type. Not all printers will reflect this when the document is printed out.

indents: Set the line spacing and indentations for selected areas of text, indicated by brackets on the screen.

menu bar: A list of commands arranged horizontally on top of the screen which can usually be pulled down for additional commands.

message line: A line on the bottom of the screen that gives you information about the program.

margins: The strip of blank space around the edge of the paper.

open: To bring a file on screen that was previously saved.

print: The command to print a document (produce a hard copy).

ruler: The line running across the page showing the tabs and margins of the document can be turned on or off.

save: To copy a file from the computers temporary memory to a more permanent storage on a hard disk or floppy.

save as: To save a file under a different name. It can also be used to save a file to a floppy. Example: Save As: **A:victor**, would save a file to the A drive as **victor**.

tabs: A tab stop is a point in the document where the cursor will stop after the tab key is pressed. Standard tab settings are every 5 spaces. Each time the tab key is hit, the cursor moves 5 spaces.

underline: This command turns on a function that will underline letters or words as you type.

<Pg Dn> A key that will move the cursor down a full page.

<Pg Up> A key that will move the cursor up a page.

F1: This is the help key for *Works*.

Microsoft Works

For the Student

One of the reasons I chose **Microsoft Works** as a word processor is that it has an excellent tutorial program. After you have glanced over the vocabulary listed above, you should work with the tutorial to obtain additional information and to solidify all the functions of word processing. If you are short of disk space, you do not need to load the tutorial on hard disk, but merely put it in the proper drive (usually A:) and use it from there. The following operational guide for the tutorial will be based upon using a floppy disk.

Using the Tutorial

Place the floppy disk labeled Tutorial in the A: drive
(Note: Because there is a lot of information on it, the floppy is a 1.2 MB high density disk)

1. At the **C:>** prompt, type **A:** press <Enter> to get to the A drive

2. When the **A:>** prompt appears type in the word A:>**Learn** and press <Enter>

3. Type in your first name and press <Enter>

4. Press the <Pg Dn> key.

5. Type in **W** for Word Processing.

6. Follow the instructions on the screen.

To Start the Program

To begin using the Microsoft Works program, follow these steps:

1 Move the lightbar down to **Word Processing** and press <Enter>.

2. Use the mouse to click on the **Word Processor** icon.

3. Press the <Alt> key or use the mouse to pull down the File menu.

4. Click **New** if you are using the file for the first time.

Or

5. Click **Open** if you have a file that you have previously saved and now want to use.

6. Use the arrows to move to **Word Processing** and press <Enter>. The word processing screen will appear.

```
ILLUSTRATION OF THE WORD PROCESSING SCREEN
*****************************************************************
File      Edit      Print     Select    Format    Options    Window

New       Undo      Print                          Check
Open      Move                                     Spelling
Save      Copy
Save As   Delete
Close
Dos
Exit
```

Writing a Letter

A simple letter will serve as an example to illustrate the functions of word processing.

1. Press <Enter> three times to move the starting point down from the top.

2. Hit the **tab key** 9 times to move the starting point over to where you want to type in the date.

3. Type the date in desired format (**3/3/93** or **March 3, 1993**.)

4. Press <Enter> three times to move down three lines.

5. Type the salutation, **Dear Jane:**

6. Press <Enter> twice. Press <Tab> once and start the letter. Note that the cursor returns to the beginning of the line automatically when you complete a line.

7. Type the following sentences:

This is the ffirst time I am writtingg a letter on the computer. This will not be a very long letter and I will make many miskakes. <Enter>

My name is (type in your name) **I am in the** (type in grade level) **grade at** (put in school name).

The letter will now look like this:

March 3, 199x

Dear Jane,

This is the ffirst time I a m writtingg a letter on the computer. This will not be a very lon letter and I will make many miskakes.
My name is Jack. I am in seventh grade at Mark Twain Jr HS.

Insert, Delete and type over

1. Move the cursor to the right of the n of **lon.**

2. Type **g** The program will insert the letter g and move everything over.

3. Move the cursor under the first f of **ffirst.**

4. Press the < Del > key. This will delete the letter and move all the other letters.   (You can also use the backspace key to delete a letter to the left of the cursor.)

5. Move the cursor to the first letter of your name.

6. Press <Ins> to activate the type over. The bottom line of the screen will show **OVR**

7. Type Fred. Notice that the word Fred types on top of your name. If you are rewriting a section you might want to use this feature but be careful or you may overwrite text you want to keep.

Mark, Bold Underline and Delete

1. If you want to select a word to bold, delete or underline move the cursor to the first letter of the word and press **F8** twice. (to select a **sentence** press f8 three times.)

2. To bold the word press <Ctrl> and hit **B**

3. To underline the word press <Ctrl> and hit **U**

4. To delete press <Del>

Check Spelling

1. Press <Alt> to access the menu bar.

2. Use the arrows to select **Options**.

3. From the options menu, select **Check Spelling**.

4. Any misspelled words are displayed in the Spelling dialogue box.

5. Select from the following basic options:

Replace the word with the correctly spelled word.

Ignore this instance of the word. Press <Alt> +I

Ask **WORKS** to suggest some other spelling for the word.

Select a word from the list of suggestions. Press <Alt> +C to change the word.

The spell checker will pull out the word "miskakes."

Save the letter (file)

To save a file the first time:

1. Press <Alt> to access the menu bar.

2. From the menu bar, select **File.**

3. From the File menu select **Save.**

4. Enter a file name (not more than 8 letters) in this case **letter1.** (Spaces between characters are not allowed.)

To save a file after the first time:

1. Press <Alt> to access the menu bar.
2. From the menu bar select **File.**
3. From the file menu select **Save.**

The file is now saved. This should be done frequently.

Save As

Sometimes you may want to save two versions of the same letter or an in between step. To do this you use the **Save As** command.

> 1. Press <Alt>.
>
> 2. Select **File.**
>
> 3. Select **Save As.**
>
> 4. Input the name for the second version of the file such as Letter2.

Close file   To close the current file and remove it from the screen:

> 1. Press <Alt>
>
> 2. Select **File**
>
> 3. Select **Close**

If you have made any changes since your last save, **WORKS** asks you if you want to save the changes. Select Yes or No.

This completes the first set of exercises for the **WORKS** word processor.
The second set of exercises will include **open an existing file, move, copy, file, print and undo.**

Open Existing File To open a saved file:

1. Press <Alt> to access the menu bar.

2. From the menu bar, select **File**.

3. From the File menu, select **Open Existing File**. A File window appears.

4. Type the name of the file (letter1) or use your up and down arrows to highlight the name from the file list.

5. Press <Enter>. The selected file is retrieved from the hard disk and appears on the screen.
(When the file appears on the screen the original is still on the hard disk. You are only making changes to a copy of the file till you save and replace the original.)

Move or Copy To move or copy a block of text to a new location:

1. Press <Alt> to access the menu bar.

2. From the menu bar choose **Select.**

3. From the Select menu choose **Text option**.

4. Use the arrow keys to highlight the text you want to move or copy. (Text is highlighted on the screen) Using the same letter, move the cursor to the beginning of the sentence My name ... Use the right arrow key to highlight the whole sentence.

5. Press <Alt> and select **Edit.**

6. From the **Edit menu** select **Move or Copy**

Try the move first, then copy it back to its original location.

7. Move the cursor to the point where you want the information to appear. Press <Enter> and the text will be copied to the cursor location.

Undo

Undo reverses the most recent command in word processing.

1. Immediately after copying the sentence My name .... press <Alt>.

2. From the menu bar select **Edit.**

3. From the Edit menu select **Undo.**

You must use Undo immediately after you make a mistake. If you do any action before the **Undo** command you cannot reverse the mistake.

Typeover

Sometimes you may want to type over some portion of work. To do this press <Ins> and **(OVR)** will appear on your screen. When turned on, the overtype mode allows new text to type over previously existing text. When turned off (Insert mode) new text is inserted and the original text is moved to the right, remaining intact.

Printing

To print your document press <Ctrl> <P>. This creates a paper output of the work files.

1. Press <Alt> to access the menu bar.

2. From the menu bar, select **Print.**

3. At **Number Of Copies** enter the number of copies. The default is 1 copy.

4. Move the cursor to **Draft quality** if you are only going to use this copy to make corrections. (It is a good idea on a long document to print draft quality copies at various points and read them for corrections.)

5. Move the cursor to **Print Specific Pages** if you want to print only certain pages (e.g. if you want to print page 2 to 4, type 2-4. If you want to print pages 2 and 5 type 2,5.)

6. Press <Enter> or select **OK to Print.** Select **Cancel** to cancel the printing.

Exiting WORKS

To close all the files and exit to DOS or the menu:

1. Press <Alt>.

2. Select **File.**

3. Select **Exit WORKS**.

Works will not allow you to exit without confirming whether you want to save any changes that you have made since your last save.

File Management

As you continue to write letters and reports, you will build up many different files on your hard disk. Eventually you will need to do some *housekeeping*. This consists of deleting old files, copying files to floppy disks for backup and renaming some files so you will be able to recognize them. This process is called File management.

File management handles file commands such as copying, deleting and renaming files and creating and removing Directories.

Use the standard access methods:

1. Press <Alt>

2. Select **File**

3. Select **File management**

The File Management dialogue box appears: Follow the procedure on the screen.

To copy a Works file to another disk (for backup):

1. Select **Copy File.** The **Files** dialogue box will open.

2. Type the name of the file you want to copy, including the three letter extension, or move the lightbar to highlight the name of the file and press <Enter>.

3. Type the drive and name you would like to use to save the file.

Example: **A:Victor**

To Delete a File:

1. Select **Delete File.**

2. Type the name of the file you want to delete, including the three letter extension, or move the lightbar to highlight the name of the file and press <Enter>.

To Rename a File:

1. Select **Rename** File

2. Type the name of the file you want to rename, including the three letter extension, or move the lightbar to highlight the name of the file and press <Enter>.

3. Type in the new name including the three letter extension and press <Enter>.

Keyboard Shortcuts

As you get more familiar with **Works** software there are certain keyboard shortcuts that can help you on highly repetitive functions.

To select or highlight:

1. Move the cursor to the beginning of the section.

2. Press **F8** twice.

3. The next word will be highlighted

4. Press **F8** three times.

5. The following sentence will be highlighted.

Other shortcuts:

<Ctrl> <End> Goes to the end of the file.

<Ctrl> <Home> Goes to the beginning of file.

<Ctrl> <B> Applies bold to highlighted text.

<Ctrl> <U> Applies underline to highlighted text.

From Word Processing To Creative Writing

You have worked through the key examples of word processing as used in *Microsoft Works* . This will launch you on the way to being able to create school reports, letters and other forms of written communication.

Now that you are comfortable using **WORKS**, you may wonder what to write. Some students have no trouble coming up with ideas for essays or stories. Others get enough encouragement and direction in school. But, for students who need help getting started in writing, I have given some hints to stimulate creativity.

For the Parent and Student

Parents guide to helping students find topics

One method to find a topic is to come up with a series of questions that a student can answer by writing an essay. It is important that these questions be phrased so the student needs to think, and that the questions elicit more than a one sentence or, worse yet, one word answer. A request to ``write about your summer vacation'' may lead to a long travel story.  It may also lead to a one line response: ``We went to Yosemite.'' With a student suffering from premature writer's block, you'll have more success with a specific set of questions.

Some examples:

Write about how you felt while backpacking in the Sierra.

What happened when you camped for the night?

What do you hope to do the next time you go backpacking?

Asking students to describe feelings and desires will enrich their vocabulary and help them learn to draw on their memories and creativity. This process began with the picture in *Once Upon a time* and should continue here with an attempt at more abstract writing.

One way to help students develop abstract and introspective writing skills is to encourage them to keep a journal on their computer, like the one kept by the whiz kid doctor on the *Doogie Howser, M.D.* television series. As Anais Nin wrote in her famous diary, ``We ... write to heighten our own awareness of life ... We write to taste life twice, in the moment and in retrospection.'' Writing a few sentences each day as to what they did, felt or enjoyed, will develop students' writing abilities, as well as their self-discipline and sense of introspection.

In keeping a journal, students need to be encouraged to use words that describe emotions: happiness, loneliness, fear, derisiveness. Using new words from their vocabulary list will help them write about their feelings with greater depth.

Here is another method to inspire creative writing. Give the student a beginning for a story and ask for it to be completed with three different endings. Coming up with the beginning of the story requires more work on your part, but can be very rewarding. It will help the student see that in life there isn't always one pat answer.

All of these writing exercises help to develop students' writing skills. In this way, using word processing and **writing** will become a natural part of the student's day.

Chapter 14

COOPERATIVE LEARNING

To The Parents

An important facet of education is socialization. The interchange of language and ideas with peers is a key factor in the building of self esteem and the development of any student. This interchange also helps students accept different ideas as well as schoolmates.

Cooperative learning is a set of instructional strategies that uses small groups of pupils to promote peer interaction and cooperation. Academic subjects, art projects, problem solving, and developmental projects can all benefit from cooperative learning. Although this is a somewhat radical idea in education, some schools are starting to explore this new venture. In the corporate world progressive firms like IBM state "If you can't work as a team you can't work for us."

Robert E. Slavin of John Hopkins University says "There is now substantial evidence that students working in small cooperative groups can master material better than on their own." Children enjoy being with their friends. Our aim in the **Computer Curriculum** is not to discourage that friendships but to enhance children's ability to work with their peers. In school, students are encouraged to work alone, not in teams. But in the workday world one almost always shares tasks with co-workers, even working in groups to solve problems or develop new projects for the company. Cooperative learning prepares the children for these types of work environments.

Cooperative Learning in Schools

Cooperative learning has been recommended as effective in many school subjects. The problem is that not many teachers have been trained to use it. It also requires more teacher intervention -- an impossibility in most large classrooms. In addition, the row upon row setup of desks does not lend itself to this format of teaching.

One form of cooperative learning which could easily be integrated into the **Computer Curriculum** is instruction based upon the group reading of a story. Members of the group read the story to each other, answer questions about the story, practice vocabulary words and write stories on a topic related to the story using *Works* and *Word Attack Plus.* This process integrates reading comprehension, writing and language.

In addition to the structured lessons, impromptu writing sprees can be developed by having the students write for 5 minutes about anything they want, as long as they write at least one paragraph. Bear in mind that the results may be unexpected, perhaps even a bit unnerving, like when **Calvin** of comic strip fame tells his Dad why he wasn't nominated for father of the year.

The purpose of Cooperative learning is to develop social interaction, thinking skills and tap into the creative minds of the students.

In the **Computer Curriculum**, there are many instances where group or paired activities can be interesting. In **Carmen Sandiego**, one person can be the detective while others look up the information in the almanac, *Foder's Guide to the U.S* or other reference works.

In **Oregon Trail** the idea of two leaders who make joint decisions helps build a cooperative spirit. Discussion of the various alternatives builds the ability to analyze what each of the decisions imply. Having to defend a position can help clarify the thinking that goes into it.

Two worthwhile programs that are not included in the core curriculum are *Sim City* and *Civilization,* both of which require students to cooperate to make many different decisions. They are discussed later in the book.

Ideas for Cooperative Learning

Here are some team projects that you can initiate.
(Items in italics are examples)

1. Writing an Adventure Story

Objectives:

- Develop creative writing skills.

- Practice typing skills and the word processing program (Microsoft Works).

- Work with other's to develop a finished product.

Student Skill Development:

- Creative writing

- Typing

- Word processing

- Active imagination

How It Works

In this exercise, two students use the word processor to write down notes and ideas for a story. They start by making an outline of the story, then print it out. Next they create characters (using the students' names personalizes the process) and choose a topic or storyline. This, too, is printed out.

The story is written in four parts:

- Introduction and location
  (*Going for a camping trip in the Sierra's*)

- Start of the story
  (*Packing up, loading the car, forgetting the food, flat tire*)

- Main action
  (*Unpacking, setting up tents, burning the pancakes, combating very large flies*)

- Resolution or completion
  (*Having a good time, Returning home, planning to go again next year and bring a friend*)

After writing the story students would edit and rewrite it to obtain a final version.

An alternative to this is to have students write different endings to the same story or even to have each one write a different middle and end and then compare them.

2. T.V. Script writing

Objective: To write and develop a TV script for an existing show.

Student Skills:

- Typing

- Word processing

- Vivid imagination.

 TV, a major part of most Americans' lives, is a good starting point to bring out ideas in a student. It is important that the TV. show has educational value.

Activities:

- Determine which TV show will be used as a model.
(Start Trek, the next generation)

- Outline an episode or show.
(show dealing with prejudice,)

- Develop a part for each character.
(Create fictional characters. Don't forget the boy/girl angle. Why does this character have two heads? Are three hands better for scratching mosquito bites ?)

- Write the part for each character.
(Why is the character prejudiced?)

- Develop and write scripts using word processing.
(Setting, location, time etc.)

Act out the scripts.

3. Create a TV Commercial and Newspaper Ad.

Objective

- To distinguish between fact and opinion in advertising.

- To understand advertising techniques.

Student Skills

- Reading comprehension.

- Concept Analysis.

Activities

- Determine a product (real or made up).
(Dehydrated water)

- Discuss what would make a customer buy it.
(Being thirsty)

- Using **Printshop,** work up an ad for the product.
(Show the desert)

- Analyze an ad for a real product
(A luxury car advertisement)

4. Budgeting

Objective:

- To create a real budget using the computer.

Student Skills:

- Word processing

- Spread sheet software

Activities:

- Get a general overview of a budget and develop categories.

- Explain income and expenditures.

- Set up an imaginary family
(Father, mother, 4 year old child.)

- Determine type of job and approximate salary for parents.
(Bassoon player $600 per week)

- Determine cost of house/apartment.
(1/2 bedroom, 1/4 bath, large closet $950)

- Develop a grocery list for a week and shop so food costs can be determined.
(Have student do a comparative shopping run at two supermarkets)

- Buy a car on time payments.
(Have student find out interest rates and what the total cost of the car actually is.)

- Develop some credit card buying and major purchases --
refrigerator, furniture etc.
(Figure out real costs based upon credit card rate of interest)

- As a group, try to work out a balanced budget using spread sheet software.

5. Personalized Birthday Cards for Friends

Student Skills:

- Word processing.

- Creativity.

- Use of **PRINT SHOP** software.

Activities:

- Make a list of friends and their birthdays.
  (Families can be used as well)

- Use a word processing or calendar program to list the dates.

- Create a birthday card for the friends whose birthdays are coming up.
  (Develop original slogans.)

6. A Presidential Campaign
(Or governor, senator, mayor -- use whatever election is coming up)

Student Skills:

- Word processing.

- Understanding of the political system.

Activities:

- Determine the name of the candidate.
(Kant Reed, Bay B. Quissn, Mor N. Mortexes)

- Develop a biographical background for the candidate.
(Birthplace, upbringing, religion, military service)

- Determine the major issues in this election.
  (homeless, gangs, economy, education etc.)

- Develop positions for yourself as the candidate on these major issues.

- Create a "News Story" about what the candidate is saying and doing in the campaign.
  (Kissing babies and making noises with his lips)

7. Starting a Small Business

Objectives:

Understanding the computer as a management tool.

Gaining hypothetical experience managing a business.

Student Skills:

Typing

Spreadsheets

Graphics

Activities:

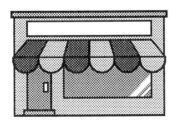
In this exercise a student or group of students writes a plan for starting a pizza restaurant. They write out a list of things they have to do to start the restaurant and then, using the spreadsheet program, prepare a start-up budget. Several students could divided the project.

Students must;

1.   Determine location and the size of the restaurant.

2.   Determine the equipment that is needed.

3.   Find out the rental cost.

4.   Find out the equipment costs.

5.   Develop the menu.

6.   Determine the hours of operation.

7.   Decide how to advertise and where.

8.   Make a to-do list to get the restaurant open.

Each of these projects has value related to education and to aspects of using the computer. The more time spent on each project, the better understanding students will have of each of the topics.

Developing Additional Ideas

These are some suggestions of projects. You can exercise your own imagination as well as your child's to develop others. The number of projects is limited only by your creativity.

In all of these projects the computer becomes an education tool and "coaching" assistant, expanding the possibilities of the peer group. These creative projects allow students to stretch their imaginations in a fun, sharing environment while developing new skills and enriching their education.

Chapter 15

Other Educational Software

For the Parent

This list of additional software meets many of my criteria for educational programs. Any program you purchase should have educational value, encourage learning and motivate the student.

Purchasing computer programs is similar to purchasing books. The easiest way to find out about new programs is to read reviews in newspapers or computer magazines, many of which are available in public libraries. An hour spent looking at software reviews will help you in finding new programs. In some of the computer software stores, the employees are familiar with software and can help guide you. In general, however, I have found that most software store employees only know the most popular software, which usually doesn't include educational programs. Explain exactly what type of software you need and make sure the store has a return policy which permits you to return programs if they don't meet your expectations.

When evaluating which software to buy, there are a number of factors to consider. The most important one relates to your computer. Ask yourself the following questions.

1. Does my system have enough memory ?

2. Is my monitor compatible with what the program needs ?

3. Do I have enough disk space to load this program ?

Most programs today require a minimum of 640k of memory. Current monitors are VGA and Super VGA or SVGA. The previous generation of monitors was EGA,

Most programs sold today will still run on them. The better programs require a lot of disk space, up to 5 million bytes of disk for a single program.   If your system has only 20 million bytes, loading this class of programs can fill up you hard disk very rapidly.

The next issue relates to the educational value and interest capturing ability of the software. Is this software useful and will it retain my child's interest? There are some programs, such as pure drill programs, which are boring, and others, with colorful graphics, that are really only games. Programs that blend graphics and other aspects to make the program interesting, while maintaining educational value, are the ones to buy.

Other Educational Software

Here are some descriptions of additional programs I have reviewed and believe you may want to consider as supplements to the **Computer Curriculum.**

TETRIS (SUPERTETRIS)

For the Parent

This family of computer games represents a highly addictive collection of fast-action brain teasers. A very popular cerebral puzzle dealing with geometric relationships plus coordination, Tetris is lots of fun. It helps a student build the ability to look ahead (by previewing the piece coming next) and in decision making as to the placement of each piece. The game strengthens depth perception and visual acuity. The faster a piece comes into location, the higher the score. This is a good computer activity with some educational benefits. This game was actually used at MIT in a study related to brain activity.

For the Student

Tetris takes place in a multi-layered pit. Geometric shapes appear at the top of the pit and begin their descent. Challengers must flip or rotate the falling geometric blocks to form solid rows. When a layer is completed it disappears leaving more room to maneuver. If the blocks reach the top of the pit, the game ends. This is a hard game to describe but is easy to play. The faster you get the blocks into place the more points you can score.

SIM CITY

For the Parent

 This is a simulation program with many very interesting concepts built in. It may be difficult to remember that you bought it for your child and not for yourself. At least make an attempt to share the program with your child rather than hogging it yourself. The program places you in the position of a mayor who is designing a city. (It really should be a city planner). You zone the land and buildings, build the power plants and determine the location of police and fire stations in order to control crime and fires. If the citizens (Sims) like the design, the city will grow. If not, they will complain to the mayor (you).

Sim City teaches students some of the real problems of city planning plus the process that occurs when politics and people's needs meet and/or conflict. It introduces the concepts of compromise and political promise in a democracy.

The program also deals with fiscal restraints relating to the tax base and a balanced budget. This is a very good way to teach financial concepts to a child. While the game can be played by some 10 year olds, the city planning has enough theory to provide an educational base for high school and college courses. Some kids under 14 will need help the first few times they play the game but, as with most good educational software, most kids will catch on very fast.

For the Student

Sim City places you in the role of a mayor who is about to design a new city. You must first learn what zoning means and then decide how you want to zone the land; for industry, housing, parks, etc. Next you build the utilities such as power plants, and connect the utility lines. Finally you must provide the essential services of police and fire stations in order to control crime and fires.

If you develop a good design, the city will grow as the citizens (Sims) move in. They will build their homes and factories, calling on you to build more roads to support their traffic needs. As a mayor you will have to decide weather to add zones and/or services as the citizens request. You will also become sensitive to all sorts of costs, planning the city growth based on tax and income, as well as the Sims' demands. Constrained by the tax income you will have to budget where you want to spend your money.

This game appears easy at first, but, as you learn more about creating a city, you will realize the many factors that go into it. Every city is unique; the designs will respond to your effort. In the end, you will appreciate the complexity and interest in the development of a city.

The Children's Writing and Publishing Center

For the Parent

The Children's Writing and Publishing Center is an introductory word processing program that includes a number of desktop publishing features. In easy steps students learn the program and create stories, letters and fliers. I have some reservations about the program for any child older than 12 as it does not include a spell checker. However, if your student has problems learning the regular word processing program, this could be an easy introduction to it.

For the Student

This program will help you produce letters, fliers, and reports along with some graphics to enhance presentation. It is very easy to learn and has simple pull-down menus and screen prompts. About 150 graphics are included in the package, which can be inserted anywhere in a letter or report.

HEADLINE HARRY

For the Parent

As parents, we often forget that our children did not live through the Vietnam war and may know very little about the Kennedy assassination. Headline Harry teaches them about these and other events in contemporary history. It also guides the student through the process of research. Starting with the gathering and recording of information, and adding the concept of including other sources for additional information, Headline Harry is a good decision making program that will teach kids history. But, more important, it will impart a message about historic method to them. Sorting out the facts requires careful reading. Since it's a little harder work than some of the Carmen programs, in the beginning you may hear kids say: ``I don't like this program.'' Often, however, students will be drawn into the story and learn many things.

This is also a good game for the ``team learning'' concept. A small group of students can enjoy the program at the same time. It will be useful to have some reference material available when questions about geography and history come up.

For the Student

As a cub reporter for the U.S. Daily Star, your mission is to find the key elements of the lead story. You will travel through the country and time, talking to people (conducting interviews), listening to the radio and checking references (reading) in order to put together a story and meet the deadline. You can also use the phone to call for information. During the game, some questions about geography or history appear and you earn more time to complete the story if you answer correctly.

As you turn in each story, you get a promotion and earn a new area of the country to cover. The ``boss'' has another goal. He wants to put the rival paper, *The Diabolical Daily*, out of business. The faster you complete accurate stories, the better the circulation figures for the *US. Daily Star* become.

WORD ATTACK PLUS IN SPANISH

and WORD ATTACK PLUS IN FRENCH

Depending on your method of learning a foreign language, these programs could be useful for vocabulary enhancement. While these programs are the same as the English version, they are not quite the same as developing vocabulary in your native language.

PC GLOBE

For the Parent

PC Globe, an electronic atlas with detailed facts, figures and instant profiles all available as a single source, is more of a reference tool than an educational software game. If you travel as a family, it will be useful for your children to look up the countries where you will travel. A good source for any information relating to current news, it can be very useful for school reports as well. Some kids even get hooked on geography and decide to look up all the facts about certain countries. Others become fascinated by the multi-colored flags, or by the currencies used in various countries. It is hard to determine what in this program will attract your children but there is always something they will find fascinating.

For the Student

This program can be very useful when you need any type of geographic information about a country. It includes lakes, rivers and mountains along with a great deal of information relating to natural resources and economic factors. Information about a country's leaders is also included. Once you start using this program you will find it useful at many different times.

CIVILIZATION

For the Parent

Civilizations is another decision-making game in which students can learn both history and the effect of technology on society. Starting at the dawn of recorded history -- 4000 B.C. students nurture their society through technological discoveries against competing civilizations. The competing civilizations are guided by history's legendary figures, such as Alexander the Great, Napoleon and Julius Caesar.

For the Student

As you use this program to develop your own civilization, you will discover new technologies including the wheel, the alphabet, navigation and nuclear weapons. You will build the wonders of the world, including the Pyramids and the Great Wall. Every economic, political and military decision is yours, from population growth to industrial policy. The destiny of civilization is in your hands.

The Engine of Life (A Human Heart Tutorial)

For Parents

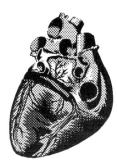

It is easy to forget how miraculous the human heart is. Hidden in the middle of your chest protected by your breastbone and backbone, the muscles of you heart perform constant labor. The Engine of Life shows the heart from a fresh perspective. It displays the functions of the veins which carry blood to the heart, the four chambers which contract to keep the blood flowing, the valves which open in only one direction to keep the blood flowing in the right direction, the arteries, which carry blood away from the heart and the sequence of events of each heartbeat, known as the cardiac cycle. In addition it teaches about the conduction system, the EKG and what it means to have a heart attack. Anyone completing this program will, better understand the functions of the heart.

For the Student

This will be probably be your first introduction to the human heart. I am sure you will find it fascinating to learn how it works and why it is so important. When you read in the newspaper about someone having a "heat attack" you will be able to understand the physiology of the process.

Summary:

The above are just a few of the better education programs available today. New and better programs are created every day. With the foundation you and your student have built using the computer curriculum, integrating such programs into the curriculum should be fun, easy and of course, educational.

Chapter 16

What We Have Learned

For the Parent

With this book as a guide, you will help your children along the path of computer literacy. At the end of this journey they will have enhanced their basic knowledge of math, vocabulary and geography while improving their ability to write, research and communicate. With these skills behind them, they can look forward to future success in school.

The subjects your children will master can help them do well on standardized tests. But, more importantly, critical thinking skills will open their minds to creative processes and decisions making. The ability to begin to think for themselves will serve them well, not only in school but in the workplace, in social interaction and in all the situations they will face in life.

Those students who work with the **Computer Curriculum** always improve their standard test or PSAT scores, which is useful for being accepted to Colleges or Universities. However, the real paradigm shift is more difficult to quantify. Some of the actions you will observe after your student has worked with this program will show the real differences. A student who had a hard time producing a one-page hand-written essay should be able to use a word processing program to write a three-page essay with perfect spelling. Any school that emphasizes academic objectives will recognize the merit of such progress. A student who suffered math-phobia, cringing at the very mention of algebra, should be able to work quadratic equations correctly and, hopefully, even understand what the process is doing. A student whose knowledge of computers was limited to video games should be able to work with a PC every day, probably understanding it better than most adults. The sense of accomplishment brought on by hard work will leave students empowered, with underlying faith in their ability to achieve personal and educational goals. This end result is not quantifiable, yet holds more value than any test score.

New Role for Parents in Education

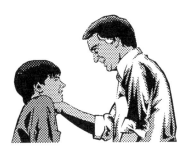

Education has always been, and will continue to be, a family affair. For thousands of years, a son has been educated by his father or grandfather and a daughter by her mother or grandmother. As Robert Bly says in *Iron John*: ``The traditional way of raising sons, which lasted thousands of years, amounted to the father and sons living in close proximity while the father taught the son a trade: perhaps farming or carpentry.'' Today this is no longer possible. The father goes off to work at something the son doesn't understand, disallowing the father/son bond. In many homes the mother also leaves to go to work at an occupation her daughter does not relate to. With both parents working full-time outside the home, the traditional role of parents in education has been diminished. In this program I have provided a way to use modern technology to reintroduce that important parent/teaching role into the home.

I have also discussed some of the deficiencies of both public education and our framework for education in general. This program of supplemental education cannot replace a good school system, but it can help students get the most out of their classroom experience.

Education cannot be relegated only to the schools. Even if the schools were excellent and staffed with wonderful teachers, the role of the parent as educator could not be neglected. Parents are at-home educators. As such, they can both directly and indirectly affect the intellectual development of young students. It is only in a partnership between the home and the school that a total system of education can be provided.

The **Computer Curriculum** can help foster greater dialogue between you and your child. I have found that this program is an educational experience for both students and the parents. You, as a parent, will become more cognizant of some of your child's thinking processes and preferences by communicating on a twice-weekly basis in a very positive manner.

SUMMARY

How Students Benefit

This program will enhance learning by providing students with the technological tools and the guidance to develop higher level skills. They are given stimulating experiences appropriate to their level of ability, including those that are necessary for success in tomorrow's workplace.

These skill include:

1.   Mastery of basic computer technology.

2.   New writing and visual communication skills.

3.   Higher-level reasoning, problem solving and critical thinking skills.

4.   Positive study skills and an increased love for learning.

5.   Development of effective traits such as confidence and self-esteem.

6.   Better ability to work in a collaborative mode.

7.   Improved scores on standard tests.

This program will also establish the foundations for life-long learning through improvement in educational skills and development of student motivation. It will help make learning fun.

This can be shown by:

1. Increased time spent in learning activities at home.

2. Decreased time spent in front of the television.

3. Increased motivation and a positive attitude towards education.

4. Better self-esteem and a sense of empowerment, making all tasks easier to handle.

How Parents Benefit

This program will help foster a dialogue between you and your child. In the process of developing this program, I have found that it promotes greater use of the computer in the home. Families discover the wealth of software available. Those family members who previously had no interest in the computer may find themselves using it. One recent study in Indiana schools found that when one child in a family was using a home computer, everyone else in the family began to use it also. The study concluded that, ``The home computers were used regularly by three-fourths of the mothers, one-half of the fathers, and most siblings who could read." This program can help develop the parent-child bond that is lacking in many families today and bring the family together around the computer.

Where Do We Go From Here?

Every contemporary society talks about the status of education. The discussion ranges from Japan, where the government plans to put a computer on the desk of every high school student in Tokyo by the year 2000, to the United States, where we are still searching for solutions. But, in all of the debates about education, there is never any question that the computer will be central to educational reform and to the changes that will happen in our information-age society.

What kind of student should our educational system produce for the information-age? Not one who learns facts, dates and names by rote, but rather a student who has a genuine understanding of a discipline and knows how to use all the information-age tools to obtain data, formulate ideas and create solutions to a variety of problems. The integration of the basic skills developed in the **Computer Curriculum** -- the vocabulary in *Once Upon a Time*; group cooperation in *Carmen Sandiego*; the development of a storyline in *Microsoft Works,* are all skills needed for daily living.

The comprehensive software that integrates all of these skills into a meaningful interactive curriculum has not been written. We are still forced to take bits and pieces and put them together ourselves. This is far better, however, than what happens in the schools where the relationship between disciplines is barely emphasized and students rarely get a sense of how component parts fit into the whole picture. From the student's perspective, the only relationship between reading and writing may be that they are both taught in the same classroom on the same day. In some respects, the one room schoolhouse with one teacher had an advantage in that all the disciplines were integrated. The day will soon come when all disciplines can again be integrated using new technologies. [In the business world software such as Microsoft Works, integrates word-processing (sending a message), spreadsheets (economics or math), graphics (pictures or illustration) and on-line services (communication)]. A curriculum integrating reading, writing, history and math can accomplish its objectives by permitting a student to understand some of the structure of society and its relationship to education. When that software appears, your student will be ready for it.

Thinking, People and Computers

In working with and teaching others to work with computers, I have found that most people do not know how to utilize them to accomplish their goals. Although one sees many people sitting in front of, working with a computer, they are not really taking advantage of the computer and the powerful software that is available. I am not saying they don't know the technical aspects of the computer and software, but stating that they have not stopped to redefine their objectives and determined the best way to use the computer to achieve them.

I, too, fell into this trap. When I first started using computers for education, my goal was to teach kids vocabulary, typing and math. This was a very worthwhile project, but, as the program developed, I realized that my real goals were to educate these students for the next century. My original objectives, based upon the 19th century little red school house, needed to be redefined. When I restated my goals, I realized that education was more than vocabulary, typing and math. It included reading, writing, problem solving and research. Based upon this realization, I re-evaluated the software and changed the structure of my teaching methods. Then I went back and looked at how the computer and software could help me in achieving my redefined goals. By taking what might at first have appeared as a backward step, I was able to gain perspective and see how to better utilize the power of the computer.

Where Will the Future Lead Us?

As education becomes a focus in the US., the integration of information systems and education will be the evolutionary outcome. People will write integrated software packages for education that will combine science, economics, history, reading and math. We have the technology. Now we must strive to incorporate it into our educational system.

Some developments you can look forward to in the near future:

Multimedia

Multimedia is an integration of video, text and sound on the computer along with the capability of random access to information. This technology shows great promise for education, industrial training and many other fields. The ability to look up a certain animal, see it running through the jungle, hear its roar, study its physical characteristics and see its demographic habitat is an example of what can be done. This is far more exciting than reading a dry encyclopedic description. What can and will be done with this media is limited only by the imagination of the educational software developer.

CD ROM (compact disk, read only memory)

CD stands for compact disk, ROM stands for Read Only memory. You cannot *write* to this device, only access the information that was previously put onto it. This device can store a tremendous amount of information, one CD ROM can hold an entire encyclopedia of information. What does this mean to the student? Very little today because not enough software has been developed to make this type of hardware worthwhile. This situation is rapidly changing. There is a limited encyclopedia available on CD ROM as well as some lovely work on animals by National Geographic. You can also get all of Shakespeare, Sherlock Holmes and a wonderful series on music. While useful to teach students to do research on a limited basis, putting a textbook on CD ROM will not motivate a student to read. Any multimedia program must be a combination of text, picture and sound to stir the imagination of the "video generation."

The Compton Family Encyclopedia is often supplied with the purchase of a CD ROM drive, but the larger MultiMedia Encyclopedia is too expensive for home use. I believe that just as software has come down to reasonable levels, CD ROM will also come into an affordable range as demand and volume increases.

On-line Services

On-line services are information bases stored on large computers that you can access with your PC. By using a modem and a telephone line, you can dial into these data bases. Various on-line services such as Prodigy and CompuServe seem to offer a lot but, as yet, they have not really found a way to create a worthwhile educational data base. At the present time, the limited offerings of On Line services were not enough to warrant a section on them.

This Is Only the Beginning

This book has opened a Pandora's box for students. Its end is really the beginning. Whether your child's interest is in coins, music, chess or the scientific theory of chaos, there are programs that let you explore many subjects and work with new and interesting concepts. Whether as an auto-technician diagnosing fuel injection problems or as a bank president forecasting financial futures, in the 21st Century your child will be using a computer

Clearly, the future belongs to the computer literate.

Congratulations! You have taken the first step to prepare your child for the 21st century.

APPENDIX A

A group of systems to establish guidelines for which computer to purchase.

SYSTEM A:

This system is at the middle of the scale today and is very cost effective. It is not at the technical or cost frontier. If you want the latest and fastest, you have to read the monthly journals to keep up with development.

Computer: A 386-20 or 33 (20 or 33 refers to megahertz speed of the processor. Remember, more is better.)

Memory: I recommend 4 MB (megabytes) of memory. This measures the amount of program data the computer can hold in its electronic memory

Monitor: VGA or Super VGA and the corresponding video card.

Keyboard: A full-function standard keyboard is important. It should include a set of arrow keys, separate from the number keys, and a set of command keys (Ins, Home, Pgup, etc.) to the right of the regular alpha numeric keys. (This does not apply to the portable computers. See the special section on portables.)

Mouse: When I first started working in computers I couldn't see any reason for having this strange little animal sitting on my desk. But, when I began working with the Apple Macintosh, I started to see the usefulness of being able to get around the screen without wearing out the arrow keys. Today, I consider a system without a mouse incomplete. To really get full use out of the education programs, you need to have a mouse.

Two of the best mice are the ones from Microsoft and Logitec. Many lesser known brands are also very good. I recommend, however, not to buy the cheapest mouse on the block. You will be using the mouse a great deal and some of the off-brands do not feel right.

Hard Disk: At least 60 MB, 100 MB would be preferable.

Floppies: 5 1/4 " A drive and 3 1/2 " B drive.

Printer: A 24 pin dot matrix is preferable. (A pin is the point that strikes the paper. A 24 pin printer means that each letter is composed of 24 dots. The more pins, the better the quality of the documents you print.)) If price is a key consideration, then a 9 pin with graphics capability is acceptable. Two of the largest printer manufacturers are Epson and Panasonic.

As an alternative for the better systems, I recommend an inkjet or laser printer. The Hewlett Packard Deskjet has become the standard of the industry. Laser printers are also becoming more and more affordable. A laser printer is a real asset in the desktop publishing of newsletters and flyers.

Soundboard: Unfortunately, most PCs (not politically correct but personal computers) are built with the world's worst speakers. The better educational software has sound capability not only music but pronunciation in vocabulary, spelling and foreign language. A good soundboard will allow you to take full advantage of these software features. I recommend this as a desired option. However, it is not a first priority the way a mouse is. One of the best soundboards is called *Sound Blaster*. It has become the standard of the industry. It delivers a full range of audio features including digitized voice capability and microphone input.

Speakers: Along with the sound board, you will need amplified speakers. As with stereos, speakers vary tremendously in price depending on the fidelity you want. For most applications the low-end is very adequate.

SYSTEM B:

When I started writing this book, a computer based on a 286 microprocessor with one megabyte of memory was considered a reasonable system. Today, with the continual drop in prices and the fast growth of machines based on the newer and more powerful 486 microprocessor chips, a 286 machine is a somewhat doubtful choice. If price is a major consideration, take a look at:

Computer: 286-16 (16 indicates the speed measured in megahertz)

Memory: 640 k (kilobyte) or 1 MB (megabyte).

Screen: VGA is the standard today. If you're buying a used computer EGA is acceptable.

Mouse: The same as we recommended for SYSTEM A. (see description above.)

Printer: A 24 pin dot matrix printer.

System C:

Computer: A 486-25

Many computer salespeople will want to sell you a 486 computer, telling you that no one is buying 386's anymore. This is overkill. At this time, I have not seen any educational software that will run only on a 386 and not a 286, and certainly no programs that require a 486. If the path of software development continues at the present rate, it will be another three to four years before educational software that will only run on a 486 becomes available. At that point in time I expect other changes to also to appear in computer systems, such as CD ROM (compact disk read only memory) and NTSC (television). That would be the time to upgrade your computer. Today, I see no reason to buy a 486 for the purposes of this book. However the price difference between 386's and 486's is fairly small and you may want to invest for the future.

PORTABLE: A portable computer is very useful. However, for most of the projects we will be doing, a desktop is preferable. If you are going to buy a portable, I would recommend the following basic systems.

1. Under $1000 A 286 with at least 40 MB hard drive, 1 MB memory and a built in 3.5" floppy.

2. Under $2000 A 386 with a 60 MB drive, 4 MB memory and built in 3.5" floppy.

SUMMARY

In this section I have described three different sets of hardware. There are many more choices available but these are representative of a low end, a mid-range system and a portable, all of which will meet your student's needs.

Putting the Computer Together

Take the computer out of the box, but retain the box and all of the packing equipment because, if something is wrong, you will have to take it back, or send it back to the seller.

Separate the warranties from the other literature, fill them out and mail them as soon as possible. Find a packing list or parts lists and check off each item to be sure you have and understand what everything is. This is especially important with printer cables. You should at least have a computer case, a monitor and its cable, a power cord, a keyboard and its cable. You should now take a look at the cable connectors and the back of the computer and familiarize yourself as to where each of the connectors will go. You will have round connectors, 25 pin connectors and maybe some nine pin connectors. Determine which ports each of the connectors will go in before starting assembly.

At this point, you are ready to start setting up your computer. As different computers hook up slightly differently, I will now release you to the mercy of the computer manufacturer's manual. They have improved tremendously in the last few years and you should have very little trouble assembling your system

APPENDIX B:

This appendix contains the information for administering the tests for *Mathblaster* and *Word Attack Plus*.[1]

Word Attack Plus

The Vocabulary test for *Word Attack Plus* contains two pages of twenty four words each. Beginning at level 1, words are listed with four possible definitions. (see example below). Students should select the best possible definition for each word. If the student finds the questions at a certain level too difficult to answer the test may be terminated at that point.

1. **abundant**   A   suggesting danger
   (Level 1)   B   thick, crowded
                     C   more then enough
                     D   threatening

After the student has completed the test, mark the incorrect answers. The first level at which the student answers two or more questions incorrectly is his/her starting level. Using this method, the level students begin at will not be too difficult for them. As a result, their progress should be encouraging.

---

[1] It is not necessary for students to take these tests. They can begin any program at any point that seems the correct level. Scores on the first section of *Vocabulary Blaster Plus* or *Math Blaster plus* will show if that is the correct level. Students scoring more than 80% should begin at a higher level, while those scoring less than 80% should begin at a lower level.

TEST FOR WORD ATTACK PLUS
LEVEL 1

1. abundant
   a suggested danger
   b thick, crowded
   c. more then enough
   d threatening

2. rigid
   a to do with cities
   b stiff and firm
   c suggesting danger
   d quick moving

3. prank
   a an equal
   b a playful trick
   c a long journey
   d a person who sells things

4. bouquet
   a a little hill
   b a bunch of flowers
   c a piece of clothing
   d something owed

5. hoard
   a to burn slightly
   b to damage
   c to store secretly
   d to hold tightly

6. cling
   a to desire something
   b to begin a fight
   c to promise seriously
   d to hold tightly

LEVEL 2

7. powerless
   a not well known
   b easily bent
   c weak
   d not fulfilling

8. anxious
   a wise and proper
   b worried
   c very weak
   d eager, desiring strongly

9. ambitious
   a unkind treatment
   b a time limit
   c a desire for success
   d substitute

10. column
    a possible harm
    b unkind treatment
    c a definite area
    d a pillar or post

11. simplify
    a to ask advice
    b to finish
    c to make easier
    d to make smile

12. vanish
    a to promise
    b to disappear
    c to guide a ship
    d to make difficult

LEVEL 3

13. portable
   a to approve
   b moveable
   c to argue pointlessly
   d to change

14. lenient
   a to divide into shares
   b tolerant, mild
   c to surround
   d to respond to

15. incinerator
   a a waste burner
   b to divide into shares
   c to treat tenderly
   d to respond to

16. cascade
   a to surround, capture
   b a small waterfall
   c to respond to
   d to join together

17. quibble
   a to approve
   b to change
   c to argue pointlessly
   d to respond to

18. confide
   a to divide into shares
   b to treat tenderly
   c to tell as a secret
   d to respond to

LEVEL 4

19. portion
   a to divide into shares
   b to treat tenderly
   c a picture of a person
   d to respond to

20. besiege
   a surround capture
   b to respond to
   c to join together
   d to quarrel

21. manor
   a a part of a hundred
   b a quantity or amount
   c a large estate
   d sending away

22. drudgery
   a story of ones life
   b loud noise
   c hard tedious work
   d a bunch

23. unruly
   a unable to be parted
   b belonging to the cities
   c germ killing
   d hard to control

24. opaque
   a unusual
   b poisonous
   c not transparent
   d improper

LEVEL 5

25. eminent
   a joyful
   b plentiful
   c unfit to eat
   d. distinguished

26. hostile
   a unfriendly
   b harmful
   c easy to read
   d a hotel

27. memento
   a a type of cheese
   b without pity
   c a souvenir
   d changeable

28. tributary
   a serious
   b an emptying stream
   c a speech
   d reckless

29. intensify
   a to manage
   b to wander
   c to make stronger
   d to go ahead

30. petrify
   a to make into stone
   b to burn slowly
   c to reject
   d to make clean

LEVEL 6

31. affluent
   a helpful
   b waterway
   c wealthy
   d very earnest

32. dubious
   a helpful
   b independent
   c careless
   d doubtful

33. eloquence
   a a skilled workman
   b a story
   c fine speech
   d a fine dress

34. sanctuary
   a a place of safety
   b a bird coup
   c a container
   d a journey

35. abhor
   a to overturn
   b to detest
   c to invent
   d to examine

36. excavate
   a to make angry
   b to annoy
   c to visit briefly
   d to dig out

LEVEL 7

37. copious
    a slightly sour
    b to take many notes
    c plentiful
    d hooked

38. nebulous
    a full of fun
    b throaty
    c part of a galaxy
    d indistinct

39. sanctum
    a a cave
    b military arms
    c a sacred place
    d idol worship

40. ennui
    a handyman
    b boredom
    c a group of three
    d the remains

41. beguile
    a to force out
    b repayment
    c to humble
    d to trick

42. pervade
    a to bury
    b to withdraw
    c to spread throughout
    d to interchange

LEVEL 8

43. adroit
    a ridiculous
    b skillful
    c futile
    d ancient

44. futile
    a out of date
    b dealing with future
    c strange
    d useless

45. tedium
    a boredom
    b repayment
    c an after effect
    d a clever remark

46. facade
    a a mixture
    b an after effect
    c front of a building
    d the finish

47. expiate
    a to figure out
    b to make amends for
    c to be overly fond of
    d to spread out

48. placate
    a to make use of
    b to soothe, pacify
    c to bring back to life
    d to scold harshly

Math Blaster Plus

The mathematics test consists of thirty-five problems starting with multiplication and ending with percentages. Math Blaster plus has six levels in multiplication and division. This test starts with multiplication and division at the highest level (6).[2]

Example:

$$8 * 9 = ?$$

Students should start the test at question 1 and continue until the problems become too difficult. After they finish, mark the test. Students should begin the program at the subject and level where they answered two or more problems incorrectly.

For example: If the student completes problem # 20 but misses #22 and # 24 then the appropriate starting point would be **FRACTIONS** (Subject) and Level 4.

---

[2]See Chapter 9 on Math Blaster Plus for definitions of levels.

MATHEMATICS　　　　TEST

******	MULTIPLICATION				FIND SUM, REDUCE	LEV 3
1	7 * 9 =	LEV 6		16	1/3 + 2/3 =	
2	11 * 9 =			17	1/5 + 3/5 =	
3	12 * 9 =			18	5/6 - 1/6 =	
4	12 * 11 =			19	1/8 + 1/8 =	
5	7 * 8 =			20	5/8 + 1/8 =	
******	DIVISION	LEV 6			DECIMALS	LEV 4
6	132/12 =			21	100 * .11 =	
7	66/11 =			22	10 * .09 =	
8	44/11 =			23	100 * .3 =	
9	72/12 =			24	10 * .13 =	
10	99/11 =			25	100 * .009 =	
******	FRACTIONS, PERCT DECIMALS				PERCENTAGES	LEV 5
	TO LOWEST TERM	LEV 1				
11	6/9 =			26	1% * 110 =	
12	10/16 =			27	10% * .09 =	
13	4/10 =			28	1% * 90 =	
14	3/9 =			29	10% * 90 =	
15	4/8 =			30	1% * 11 =	

	FORM INTO A WHOLE OR MIXED NUMBERS	LEV 2				
31	3/2 =					
31	9/5 =					
33	7/4 =					
34	3/3 =					
35	10/5 =					

Fill in your name and the date. Start the test on problem (1) and do as many problems as you can. Stop when the problems become too difficult and have the paper graded.

APPENDIX C

Record Keeping

When a teacher says "Sue got a score of 81% on her last math test" we might want to know what the average score was, how many children got a better grade, and what letter grade this score represents. The scores in the **Computer Curriculum** do not reflect on the student in the same manner. They are designed to measure students' progress from their base score and not against a "norm".

Record keeping is designed to provide a yardstick to measure a student's performance. Progress is what is important. The **Computer Curriculum** is designed for individual learning and this record keeping reflects individualized progress.

WORD ATTACK PLUS

At the end of each session the student should print out his/her scoreboard. The printed out record for *Word Attack Plus* looks like this.

```
Word Attack Plus            By Davidson
Scoreboard
*****************************************************************
Name          Frank Smith    Date    Jan. 15, 1993
Level                        (1)
Words                        Adjectives
Activity                      Sentence Completion
Correct                      19
Retries-Hints                11
Total                        20
   Score                     67%
```

The form for tracking WAP looks like this:

WORD ATTACK PLUS RECORD KEEPING
TYPE: nouns, adjectives, verbs

NAME: Frank Smith

   DATE: 4/17   4/23   4/25

Verbs 5
MULTI CHOICE	78%	87%	
SENTENCE COM	64%	76%	88%

MULTI CHOICE
SENTENCE COM

    Fill in the name at the top and the current date in the first blank column. The two exercises that you will be keeping track of are the **multiple choice** and **sentence completion.** These exercises exist for nine different levels and three forms of words. Each level should be recorded for verbs, nouns and adjectives. The sentence completion is much more difficult than the multiple choice, so there will probably be a gap between the scores that will change over time. At the end of each session, students should print out their record. Set aside fifteen minutes a week to record scores and give guidance as to what the student should work on the following week.

    Based on the scores shown in the example, you would suggest that this student move on to the next level of exercise. Any student scoring over 85% on a particular exercise should move on to the next level.

WORD ATTACK PLUS RECORD KEEPING

		TYPE LEVEL		nouns 1 - 9	adj	verbs				
	Date	4/17								
EXAMPLE										
Verbs 5										
Multiple choice		78%								
Sentence com		64%								
*************	Date									
Multiple choice										
Sentence comp										
Multiple choice										
Sentence comp										
Multiple choice										
Sentence comp										
Multiple choice										
Sentence comp										
Multiple choice										
Sentence comp										
Multiple choice										
Sentence comp										
Multiple choice										
Sentence comp										

Math Blaster Plus

Record keeping

Record keeping and tracking in math is to show the proficiency in basic math functions and the understanding of some of the more difficult concepts such as fractions and percentages.

The key program to track is ***Rocket Launcher***, which should be recorded only in the ***solve it*** mode. While scores on ***Recycler*** and ***Math Blaster*** are not good measuring devices, the programs are important tools to develop thinking and planning skills. Improvement, however, cannot be measured by any single score.

The printed out score card for Rocket Launcher looks like this. The items that are to be recorded in score keeping are Subject, Level, and Score.

```
Math Blaster Plus                    By Davidson
**************************************************
    Scoreboard
**************************************************
    Name              Jack
    Date              Aug. 25, 1992
    Subject           Fractions, Decimals
    Level             1
    Activity          Rocket Launcher
    Correct           20
    Total             25

    Score             80%
```

MATHBLASTER PLUS RECORD KEEPING

NAME										:
		TYP								
		LEV		1 - 9						
EXAMPLE:	Date	4/17								
SUBJECT:		ADD	ADD	ADD						
LEVEL		3	3	4						
SCORE		78%	86%	61%						
DATE										
SUBJECT:										
LEVEL										
SCORE										
DATE										
SUBJECT:										
LEVEL										
SCORE										
DATE										
SUBJECT:										
LEVEL										
SCORE										
DATE										
SUBJECT:										
LEVEL										
SCORE										

To keep track of Rocket Launcher. Fill in the student's name at the top and the current date in the first blank column. This exercise has six subjects and four levels. At the end of each session, students should print out their records. Set aside 15 minutes a week to record scores and give guidance as to what to work on the following week.

Based on the scores shown in the example, the student would repeat level 4 for addition. Addition and subtraction, or multiplication and division can be mixed. At any point when they score over 85% students should go to the next exercise.

Mavis Beacon Typing

The key to good typing is speed and accuracy. Fortunately accuracy today is not as important as in the past. With word processing and spell checking, typos are corrected quickly and easily. So, speed becomes the main skill.

Mavis monitors students' growth constantly. The two key scores to record are WPM (words per minute) and accuracy. These appear after each session or can be reviewed by checking the students' graphs. (See Chapter 12)

The record keeping form :

NAME										:
EXAMPLE:	Date	4/17								
WPM		12	13	15						
% ACCURACY		78%	86%	61%						
DATE										
WPM										
% ACCURACY										

APPENDIX

An example of the graph seen on the screen in Mavis Beacon Teaches Typing.

TYPING WORDS PER MINUTE

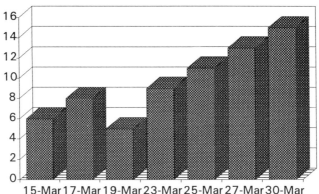

There are two levels of typing speed that are important to attain. The first is achieving 15 WPM. This is above the so called "frustration level".At this speed students start to feel they can actually write something by typing. The second level is 20 WPM at which point students can make good progress towards doing all their homework on the computer.

All records as illustrated in these three forms should be copied and three hole punched to be kept in a notebook for the students progress. File this along with the pre-computer writing sample and the three and six month records.

Bibliography

Bly, Robert. *Iron John: A Book About Men.* Reading, Mass: Addison-Wesley, 1990.

Dodge, Bernard J. "Computers and Creativity". *Communicator: Journal of California Association for the Gifted.* 21(1), January, 1991.

Fiske, Edward B. *Smart Schools, Smart Kids.* New York: Simon and Schuster, 1991.

Graham, Patricia Albjerg. *S.O.S. Sustain Our Schools.* U.S.: Hill and Wang, 1992.

Healy, James M. Ph.D. *Endangered Minds: Why Our Children Don't Think.* New York: Touchstone, 1990.

Hirsh , E.D. Jr. *Cultural Literacy: What Every American Needs to Know.* New York: Vintage Books, 1988.

Kidder, Tracy. *Among schoolchildren.* Boston, Mass: Houghton Mifflin Co., 1989.

Kozol, Jonathan. *Savage Inequalities.* New York: Crown publishers, 1991.

Margolis, Philip E. *Personal Computer Dictionary.* New York: Random House, 1991.

Marshall, Gail. "Teaching With Technology." *Communicator: Journal of California Association for the Gifted*, 21(1), January, 1991.

Mihaly Csikszentmihalyi. *Flow: The Psychology of Optimal Experience.* Cambridge University Press, 1988.

Naisbitt, John & Aburdene, Patricia. *Megatrends 2000.* New York: Avon Books, 1990.

Oakes, Jeannie & Lipton, Martin. *Making the Best of Schools.* New Haven, Conn.: Yale University Press, 1990.

Paulos, John Allen. *Innumeracy: Mathematical Illiteracy and its Consequences.* New York: Vintage books, 1990.

Polley, Paula and Wenn, Richard D. *Everything You Need to Know (But Were Afraid to Ask Kids) About Computer Learning.* Palo Alto, CA: Computer Learning Month and the Software Publishers Association. 1988. Printed in Dallas, Texas.

Slavin, Robert E. *Educational Psychology.* Englewood Cliffs, New Jersey: Prentice Hall, 3rd edition, 1991.

EDUCATIONAL SOFTWARE PUBLISHERS

Davidson and Associates, Inc.
19840 Pioneer Ave
Torrance, CA 90503

Math Blaster Plus
Word Attack Plus
Algebra
Math Blaster Mystery

The Software Toolworks, Inc.
60 Leveroni Ct., Novato, CA 94949

Mavis Beacon Teaches Typing

Microsoft Corp.
One Microsoft Way, Redmond, Wash 98052

Microsoft Works

Broderbund
17 Paul Drive
Sand Rafael, CA 94903

Where in the U.S. is Carmen Sandiego
Where in the World is Carmen Sandiego

Maxis Software
1042 Country Club Dr., Suite C
Moraga, CA 94556

Sim City
Sim Ant

Mecc
3490 Lexington Avenue North
St. Paul, Minn. 55126

Oregon Trail

The Animated Software Company
P.O. Box 188006
Carlsbad, CA 92009

The Engine of Life

PC Dynamics Inc.
31332 Via Collins #102
Westlake Village, Ca 91363

Menu Works

INDEX